FINAL SC⬤RE!

To Drew,
Know that
God is always
there for you.
when you
need Him.
In Christ,
Dan Fan

Psalm 62:6
1 Peter 5:7

DAN FARR

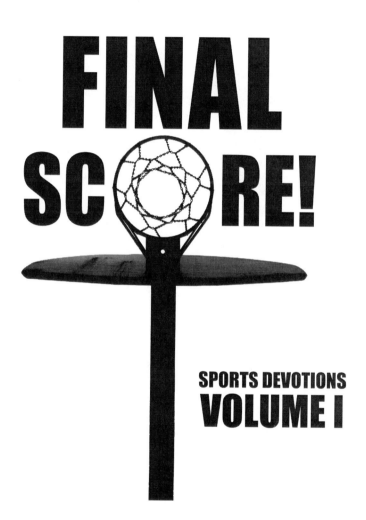

FINAL SC RE!

SPORTS DEVOTIONS
VOLUME I

TATE PUBLISHING
AND ENTERPRISES, LLC

The opinions expressed by the author are not necessarily those of Tate Publishing, LLC.

Published by Tate Publishing & Enterprises, LLC
127 E. Trade Center Terrace | Mustang, Oklahoma 73064 USA
1.888.361.9473 | www.tatepublishing.com

Tate Publishing is committed to excellence in the publishing industry. The company reflects the philosophy established by the founders, based on Psalm 68:11,
"The Lord gave the word and great was the company of those who published it."

Book design copyright © 2011 by Tate Publishing, LLC. All rights reserved.
Cover design by Kate Stearman
Interior design by Chelsea Womble

Published in the United States of America

ISBN: 978-1-61346-692-6
1. Sports & Recreation / General
2. Religion / Christian Life / Devotional
11.11.07

This book is dedicated to my wonderful wife, Becca, and our beautiful daughters, Allison and Jillian, and to my greatest teachers, coaches, and role models. This book is in honor of my father, Lester Farr, Sr., and in memory of my mother, Allene Farr, my father-in-law, Damon Ray, and Pete Maravich, whose testimony God used to change my life for eternity.

TABLE OF CONTENTS

BASKETBALL

FOOTBALL

BASEBALL

GOLF

SPORTS

INTRODUCTION

Do you know a young person (or an adult) who is crazy about sports but you can't seem to get through to them about their need for Christ? I was once that person, and God used sports at the age of forty-eight to get me to see what Christ had done on the cross for me. This book is designed to help you break through the barrier.

Through this collection of devotions and short stories, I have attempted to combine my knowledge of sports, my growing knowledge of the Bible, and everyday experiences to connect the reader to the gospel in a fresh, new way. Hopefully one of these stories will reach a young man or young woman for Christ who otherwise might have never known him.

Everyone needs to understand that it is very cool to know Jesus and for him to know us. Jesus taught the people two thousand years ago using ordinary stories about farming, water, marriage, and everyday life called parables. If Jesus wrote parables today, undoubtedly, he would toss in a few sports stories since so many people today are passionate about sports. The Apostle Paul shared with the Corinthians in 1 Corinthians 9:22, "Whatever a person is like, I try to find common ground with him, so that he will let me tell him about Christ, and let Christ save him." My hope and prayer is to share these sports-related parables in a way that the light bulb will come on for you to enable you to look at the cross as you never have before and allow God to change you and disciple you. To God be all the glory that might result from this book.

TESTIMONY

I am honored and privileged to share my testimony with you. On a Sunday morning in the late 1960s in a small Methodist church in Middle Georgia, I could have received Christ. I was drawn to Jesus Christ by the Holy Spirit during a message by a lay speaker, but I was afraid of what people would say if I went to the altar. I escaped into the warm sunshine and convinced myself that I would have enough nerve to accept Christ the following Sunday. But I went back into the wilderness for thirty-five years. I did not attend church when I moved to Atlanta, but I met my future wife, Becca, through the sports ministry at Peachtree Presbyterian Church. We married the following year and were later blessed with two beautiful daughters, Allison and Jillian. We visited Mt. Zion UMC in East Cobb, which had a new gym. Two years later, I started a basketball program and poured my energy into it for the next twelve years. It was great seeing the program grow and packing the sanctuary on basketball Sunday. But my focus was too much about personal achievement and not enough about helping young people know Christ.

I continued to live a self-centered life and could go for days without communicating with God. But in 2001, I watched the ESPN Classic special about basketball star Pete Maravich, my idol throughout high school, college, and adulthood. My vintage Maravich jersey hung in my closet for twenty-five years. I bought throwback jerseys, books, and videos on eBay. One VHS tape was Pete's testimony that I watched one Sunday night out of boredom and curiosity. That video was a divine appointment. At the time, I was drifting away from the basketball program and was very unhappy with myself. I was so far from God after many years of living without him. Jesus on the cross? It was just a story until I heard Pete tell how Christ transformed him. I always wanted to be like Pete, but I realized I wasn't because Jesus Christ knew Pete Maravich, and Jesus didn't know me. Occasionally, I wondered during sermons, *Am I going to heaven?* Then I would fool myself by falling back on my good works. But I knew that if I died that evening, I would never see Jesus face to face. I cried out in my heart that I wanted my life to change. As my former pastor, Steve Lyle, often said, "It's not the words you pray as much as the attitude of your heart."

God has blessed me with many opportunities to share my testimony. At first, I was sure I had it all figured out, but instead, there was so much to learn. God led me to turn that basketball program into our Christ-centered Hoops2Heaven ministry. I eventually allowed him to change me in the workplace when I went through trying times after a merger. An opportunity came to teach high school Sunday school and lead the basketball ministry again, which led to the start of a year-round youth sports ministry at Mt. Zion. Can you see a pattern? Youth sports ministry is my fishing hole. I continue to pray that I can get it right for Christ for our families at Mt. Zion and in our community. God loved me unconditionally, wooed me, and showed me mercy time after time until I repented, which means that I turned from my sinful ways, trusted, and obeyed. Repent, trust, and obey. There is no other way. I'm far from perfect, but God thinks I'm worth it. I was lost and then found and forgiven.

BASKETBALL

BK01:
THE HUMAN ERASER AND THE HUMAN SIN ERASER

Hebrews 10:17, Psalm 103:12

He has taken our sins away from us, as far as the east is from the west.

Psalm 103:12

The late Marvin Webster was an All-American center at tiny Morgan State University in Maryland. He later played professionally for the Seattle Sonics and the New York Knicks and helped lead the Sonics to the NBA Finals in 1978. Marvin played center, stood seven feet tall, and had an enormous wing span. He was so adept at blocking shots, sometimes achieving triple doubles in rebounds, points, and blocks, that he was nicknamed the human eraser. Marvin erased shots around the basket with such efficiency that his opponents were often intimidated.

It is noteworthy that Marvin was often seen with a Bible in his hand. Marvin's nickname reminds us of another great eraser. That eraser is Jesus Christ, whom we could call the human sin eraser. Through repentance and confession of our sins and trust in Jesus as Savior and Lord, we can have all of our sins erased as if they had never happened. As humans, we are not capable of forgetting all of the wrongs that others have committed against us. But God assures us that he will not only forgive but forget all of the times we have lied, stolen, made ourselves God, worshiped idols, and taken his name in vain. When we earnestly repent of our sins and place our trust in Christ, a supernatural event occurs. It is as if our sins were written in wax, but the wax melted and eliminated any records of our sins. Where else can we possibly receive such freedom from our past wrongdoings? Only through Jesus Christ, the human sin eraser who erased our sins on the cross, and God, Our Father, who forgives and forgets all of our sins, removing them as far as the east is from the west.

Prayer: Father God, thank you for sending the human sin eraser, Jesus Christ, to wash us as pure as snow with his crimson blood that he shed on the cross for me. Thank you for forgiving and forgetting my sins. In Jesus's holy name, amen.

BK02:
DON'T BE A BALL HOG!

Mark 9:35

Anyone wanting to become the greatest must become the least, the servant of all.

One season I was blessed with an exceptionally talented team of age nine to ten girls in our Hoops2Heaven basketball ministry. The goal is to distribute the talent as evenly as possible, but this particular season, I received more than my fair share of scorers. And scoring was exactly what most of them had in mind. I had at least four players who were capable of scoring double digits on any given day. But it was like breaking young colts to get them to pass the ball. I even tried a scrimmage where the only option to move the ball down the court was to pass with no dribbling. "No dribbling? That's hard! It's not fair!" they screamed. But they learned to move the ball quickly as a result of that drill.

I reminded them on several occasions that there is no *I* in *team*. After practice, I asked, "Now why did we do that drill tonight with no dribbling?" I expected to hear the no *I* in *team* line, but Katie quickly spoke up. "So we won't be a bunch of ball hogs!" I was satisfied that they got it, and I never brought it up again.

We're born to be a bunch of ball hogs. When things don't go our way, from the time we are two years old, we cry out in anger and rebellion. Ever notice that there is no *I* in *team* but that there is an *I* in *sin*, and *pride*, and *selfishness*? Billy Graham once said that most unrighteous anger stems from selfishness. There is only one way to remove the selfishness, and that is to turn from our self-centeredness and trust in Christ as we try to follow his way. Sure, Christ got angry, but it was righteous anger that was directed toward wrongdoing of his fellow man every time. Oftentimes, as Christians, we try so hard to conceal righteous anger that we stand and allow injustices to take place right before our eyes and we do nothing. I've been guilty more times than I care to admit.

There is no *I* in *trust, obey, love, mercy,* and *grace.* As we learn to act on righteous anger and stifle unrighteous anger, we will exhibit more and more Christlike traits. Then we won't remain a bunch of ball hogs. We will become better team players for God's kingdom.

Prayer: Father God, through the Holy Spirit living in me, please let me know when you see me being a ball hog, when I am much more concerned about myself than others. May I learn from concrete experiences so that I have fewer childish outbursts that dishonor Christians and your holy name. In the precious name of Jesus, amen.

BK03:
THE MIRACLE OF KRAIG'S
GAME-WINNING THREE

2 Samuel 9:1–13, Philippians 4:13

I can do all things through Christ who strengthens me.

Philippians 4:13

God blessed our youth sports ministry at Mt. Zion richly when he brought us a teenager named Kraig. He has as much passion for basketball as anybody in our ministry. Kraig was born several months prematurely, and the doctors predicted he would not live. He lived, but the doctors predicted he would never walk. Kraig walked, but the doctors predicted that he would not play basketball. He is a fierce competitor who doesn't let any obstacles deter him from competing and enjoying the game. Kraig plays and plays well even though some jump a little higher and run a little faster.

One Saturday afternoon, I coached a memorable game in the gym at Mt. Zion. This game was especially well played, and our team fought back from a twelve-point second half deficit. Kraig had already hit three three-pointers to bring us back. Kraig's team was down by two points with only five seconds remaining, and the opponents had the basketball. The inbounds pass flew past the top of the key, and one of our players, Ian, leaped and made a fantastic one-handed interception. Then Ian had the presence of mind to turn and find Kraig on the wing about twenty-five feet from the basket. Kraig let it fly. As the horn sounded, the ball hit nothing but net. We won! Kraig raced to the other end of the court as his mom, dad, and sister leaped out of their seats at mid-court. Kraig's teammates pummeled him with congratulations for the winning shot.

I told my Sunday school class about the winning play the next day, and there were several tears in the room, including mine. That miracle shot was a bright and shining moment, a tribute to the faith of his parents, who kept telling their son that he could do more than the doctors thought he could do. The following Monday evening, I began to prepare my Sunday school lesson about David searching for any member of Jonathan's family to join him. I received an e-mail from Kraig's mother, who described the obstacles that Kraig had overcome since birth. I then understood how special that shot was. Tears filled my eyes again. Then I said, "Oh my!" when I found out my lesson was about Mephibosheth. When King David searched for anyone from Jonathan's family to honor his covenant with Jonathan, his servant, Ziba, could only find young Mephibosheth, who could not run as fast nor jump as high as the others. Although Mephibosheth was not as physically capable as others, he had a humble heart. Because of his father's legacy, God rewarded Mephibosheth with plenty of servants and a permanent seat at King David's table in Jerusalem.

What a great and wonderful God we serve, whose perfect timing surpasses anything we can create.

Prayer: Father God, thank you for the inspiration that you sent us in the form of Kraig and the living witness he has become for all of us who are fortunate to call him son, friend, and brother in Christ. In Jesus's name, amen.

BK04:
WHAT MAKES A TEAM A TEAM?

Romans 12:3–8

Having different gifts according to the grace that is given us ...

Romans 12:6

Great teams are characterized by an excellent coach and talented, unselfish players who work as one toward a common goal. Oftentimes, there will be one outstanding player who involves his teammates very effectively, helping them play better than they would otherwise. Larry Bird and Magic Johnson, who were two of the biggest NBA stars in the 1980s, are two players who were strong leaders and brought out the best in their teammates. They were both capable of scoring many points but would pass the ball often to their teammates to get them more involved. Larry and Magic offered encouragement and constructive criticism as necessary. In turn, their teammates would show appreciation by playing even harder to win the game.

The first and second laws of the Ten Commandments teach us not to put our selfish interests above God or even equal with God. In a game, if you don't listen to your coach and instead try to do it all yourself, you will not be successful. If you try to do it yourself by hogging the ball, dribbling through three or four defenders, and taking the first shot you see from twenty-five feet, you will most likely fail, and you'll steal the joy of the game away from your teammates. But if you are centered on listening to your coach, understand what is best for your team, and play your role on the team, you will be more successful. Some of us are good shooters, some are good passers, some defend well, and some rebound well. Find out what you are good at and focus on that strength for your team.

In the early church, Paul taught that some are good at preaching, some are good at serving others, and some are good at teaching. The church is made up of many parts, and when each of us uses the special gifts that God has given us, we add to the overall effectiveness of our respective churches. If you will try to do what your coach (Jesus) teaches you and strive to help others (Mom, Dad, your siblings and friends), you will live a more joyful life.

Remember the following pecking order in sports: coach, teammates, you. Here is the pecking order in life: Jesus, others, you. Jesus, others, you makes an acronym called JOY. When the joy gets sucked out of your life, it's usually because you've reversed the order and put yourself first before God and Jesus and helping others.

Prayer: Father God, may I find joy knowing that Jesus paid the penalty for my sins by hanging on the cross, no matter what happens to me today. In Jesus's holy and precious name, amen.

BK05:
PETE MARAVICH:
LOOKING UNTO JESUS

Hebrews 12:2, James 4:14, Philippians 1:20–21

Looking unto Jesus, the author and perfector of our faith ...

Hebrews 12:2

The last day of Pete Maravich's life on this earth was January 5, 1988. Pete arrived at the Church of the Nazarene gym in Pasadena, California, to play three-on-three basketball with Dr. James Dobson, associate pastor Gary Lydic, former UCLA star Ralph Drollinger, and several friends who were eager to play basketball with the Pistol. Pete had not played basketball for months because of a sore shoulder. On the way to the gym from his hotel, Pete excitedly told Gary how God had changed him and was working in his life. Pete was in California to supervise the shooting of a movie about his boyhood life. The day before Pete left for California, he told his brother in Christ, John Lotz, that all he really wanted to do was travel across the country and tell young people how Jesus Christ had saved him and how they needed Christ in their lives.

But everything changed that morning. After a few half-court games of three-on-three, the players took a water break. Pete was shooting the ball and talking to Dobson, and Lydic was shagging balls for Pete. He told Dobson how much he loved playing basketball that morning for the first time in months. Pete's final words were, "I feel great." Suddenly, Pete collapsed and hit the floor hard face first. At first, Dr. Dobson and Gary Lydic thought he was pulling a prank. Despite twenty minutes of CPR, Pete died in the arms of Dr. Dobson in the gym.

Dobson later recalled that the T-shirt Pete was wearing the moment he went to be with the Lord bore the following words: "Looking unto Jesus."

If you die tonight, will you be looking unto Jesus, the author and perfector of our faith? God only gives us this day. Live it to the fullest, and if you haven't made Christ your Savior, I ask you, "What are you waiting on?"

Prayer: Most gracious and loving Father, help me realize that I need to live each day to the fullest for you because you give us today. Your mercies are new every morning. In Jesus's name, amen.

BK06:
SPORTSMANSHIP FOR THE AGES

Romans 8:26

The Holy Spirit helps us with our daily problems and in our praying…

My father, Lester Farr, Sr., won over eight hundred games in his high school coaching career that spanned five decades from the 1930s through the 1970s. Dad won one state championship and thirteen region championships and positively influenced the lives of hundreds of young men and women with his strong Christian character, determination, coaching skill, and strong sense of fair play. Coach Farr is ninety-eight and in good health. In fact, he has completed a loop since he was born in the tens and is now living in the tens. Despite the success that he had, he will recall the games that he lost and what he should have done differently more often than the thrilling wins.

At state tournament time each year, I am reminded that strange things happen under the bright lights and the cauldron of tournament pressure. Dad's sense of fair play was most evident in the 1952 state tournament in Macon. His Cedar Grove girls' team won the state championship in 1951 and had a great opportunity to repeat as champions. Cedar Grove trailed by one point in the final seconds when a bizarre play occurred. Following a timeout, the official incorrectly awarded the ball to Cedar Grove when the opponent should have inbounded the ball. The Cedar Grove forward drove to the basket and scored to put her team ahead. Only then did the officials realize that something was wrong.

Somewhat confused, the officials walked over to my dad and asked him what they should do. In the heat of the battle, Coach Farr surely must have thought, *You figure out the mess you made!* There was no correctable error rule in 1952 that would have reversed the points on the board. But Dad told the officials that it would be all right to take the points off the board as long as the clock was reset with the same amount of time. The opponent inbounded the ball and ran out the clock to win the game, ending Cedar Grove's chance for a repeat.

The following morning, *Macon Telegraph* sportswriter Sam Glickman wrote that Coach Farr's willingness to do the right thing, especially considering the circumstances and what was at stake for his team, was one of the finest acts of sportsmanship he had ever witnessed. It was an act of sportsmanship that surely carried over into the lives of the girls who played in the game and their friends and families who watched that evening.

Prayer: Dear heavenly Father, thank you for the legacy of Coach Farr and his integrity and for coaches everywhere who leave legacies that glorify you. In Jesus's name, I pray. Amen.

BK07: SNOOKS

Romans 2:6–10, Galatians 6:9

But glory, honor, and peace, to every man that works good…

Romans 2:10

My father-in-law, Damon Ray, or Ray as he was affectionately known throughout Hardin County, Kentucky, was a coach and principal at East Hardin High School in Glendale for many years. The school is adjacent to the football stadium, which is named Damon Ray Field. Ray passed away in May 2008, and the funeral service was very appropriately held in the gym at East Hardin High School where he was so beloved.

Although the Glendale schools had been integrated since 1956, in 1963, integration was still making its way through the South. The East Hardin High School boys' basketball team had one African American player, a young sophomore nicknamed "Snooks" Freeman. On a Friday afternoon, East Hardin traveled to Cookeville, Tennessee, to play the Tennessee Tech college freshman team on Saturday afternoon. The team would then stay overnight, play their game, and stay to watch their former classmate compete in the varsity game. But an unfortunate event occurred Friday evening. When the team checked into the hotel, the hotel proprietor told Ray that Snooks could not stay at the hotel, and that he would have to stay at a motel outside of town by himself. Ray was furious, and that evening, Ray drove his daughter, Becca, and his wife, Charlene, to Livingston, Tennessee, to stay with Becca's grandmother. And Ray brought Snooks with them.

The next day, Ray told John Oldham, the Tennessee Tech head coach, about the incident. Oldham assured him that the problem would be taken care of right away, and all of the boys were allowed to stay in the hotel on Saturday night. In another demonstration of Christian love, Oldham invited Ray and his team to his Sunday school class on Sunday morning, including Snooks. When Ray passed away, I spoke with Snooks Freeman at the funeral home. I'm confident that one reason Snooks came was because of the Christian love that Ray showed him.

The Bible assures us that we are all alike in God's eyes. "Neither Jew nor Greek, neither slave nor master…" All have the same birthright and privilege to come to know Christ. Every person on the face of this earth has had his or her sins paid for by the One who took our places upon the cross. And nobody, regardless of sex, race, or creed, will be denied heaven if that person places his or her faith in Jesus Christ as Savior and Lord.

Prayer: Father God, please teach me to love and respect everyone for who he or she is, regardless of their nationality, heritage, or the color of the person's skin. In Jesus's name, amen.

BK08:
TRIPLE THREAT

Acts 1:1–8, John 14:26, Romans 8:26

But the Helper, the Holy Spirit, whom the Father will send in My name, He will teach you all things, and bring to your remembrance all things that I have said to you.

John 14:26

One of the most important fundamental skills for a basketball player is the triple threat position. The player crouches in an athletic position with weight on the balls of the feet, which are spread slightly wider than shoulder width. The player holds the basketball firmly and tucked near the body. From this position, the player can jump and shoot, pass the ball, or dribble and drive to the basket. Those are the three options: dribble, pass, and shoot. If you watched the movie *Hoosiers*, when Jimmy made the winning basket, Jimmy was in the triple threat position before he dribbled, leaped, and scored. All expert players have mastered this fundamental skill.

Do you realize that as a child of God, you have a triple threat, the Holy Trinity, at your call every day of your life on earth? First, there is our almighty God, the Father, the maker of the universe, all powerful, all loving, who will never leave nor forsake you. Second, there is Jesus Christ, the Son of God and the Son of Man, who was born to a virgin, walked among us on earth, taught us and performed miracles. Jesus was crucified and suffered an excruciating death on the cross, but he beat the sting of death by rising from the grave on the third day. Jesus now sits at the right hand of the Father, and Jesus intercedes for you when you pray to God. Third, there is the most overlooked and most misunderstood member of the Holy Trinity triple threat, the Holy Spirit. When you receive Christ as your Savior, you are immediately and supernaturally infused with the Holy Spirit, a person living inside you. As you seek to obey God each day, the Holy Spirit helps you with your daily problems and helps you pray, even when you have no clue what to pray for or how to pray. The Holy Spirit passionately fills the prayer gaps for you so that God will understand your prayers even when you don't feel like they made sense.

Each member of the Trinity loves you more than you can ever imagine. Always remember that with the triple threat Trinity over you, by your side, and living within you, all things are possible.

Prayer: Father God, what a blessing it is to have your unconditional love. Thank you for sending your Son, Jesus, to die for me. I am grateful for the gift of the Holy Spirit to help me with my daily problems and to pray. In Jesus's name, amen.

BK09:
REPEAT OR REPENT?

Mark 1:15, Matthew 4:17

Repent, for the Kingdom of God is at hand.

Mark 1:15

When a team wins a championship, its fan base usually celebrates enthusiastically for several days. Then the question begins. Can you repeat next year? Fans don't even give teams a chance to enjoy it before clamoring for more. Fan is short for fanatic. Repeat means the team would win the championship again next year, making it two years in a row. Then if the team wins two in a row, the fans shout, "Three-peat! Three-peat!" or three in a row.

The term "three-peat" was first coined by Los Angeles Laker Byron Scott when he spoke of bringing the Laker fans three consecutive titles. In fact, Laker Coach Pat Riley later licensed the catch phrase. Ironically, the Lakers did not three-peat the following year. The next team to three-peat after the phrase was invented was the Chicago Bulls. In the late 1950s and 1960s, the Boston Celtics "eight-peated" with eight consecutive titles.

How about you? Have you ever repeated, or three-peated, or one hundred-peated, or gazillion-peated an evil action or thought? The same sin, that is. Maybe you've taken God's name in vain or lied or made yourself out to be God, or put your interests ahead of others because you think it's all about you. Either you can't shake the sin or you don't want to shake it. The Bible reminds us that there is pleasure in sin. But in the end, you need to realize that the bitterness and destruction is never worth the temporary pleasure.

Do you know that God is angry each day with unrepentant sinners who repeat the same sins over and over? Pray now that God will help you recognize specific sin and that the Holy Spirit will lead you in such a way that you will *repent* and not repeat. Just changing that one little letter from *a* to *n* makes all the difference. Turn from the sinful self that binds you and break the chains of repeat sin. Cleanse yourself through the blood of the Lamb, Jesus Christ.

Prayer: Father God, help me repent, not repeat. Show me when I mess up so that I will turn from that sin and not do it again. Please forgive me when I fall short. In Jesus's name, amen.

BK10:
KEEP YOURSELVES FROM (AMERICAN) IDOLS, LITTLE CHILDREN

1 John 5:21, Romans 3:23

Keep yourselves from idols, little children. Amen.

1 John 5:21

Many young athletes have a favorite player, a player he or she looks up to because the player is one of the best in that sport. In basketball today, two of the most popular players are Lebron James and Kobe Bryant, often referred to simply as Lebron and Kobe. My idol for many years was Pete Maravich. I rightly call him an idol because he was just that to me, much bigger and more important than God was in my life. If Pete had a great game, I was ecstatic because I knew people would say and write great things about him. If he had a bad game, I was disconsolate and moody. I admired Pete and wanted to be like him because he had these great skills and was very cool. But Pete admitted that he was no role model during his playing days because of his drinking and lifestyle. My acts of idolatry included growing a goatee like Pete, buying a jersey like Pete's, running like Pete, and trying to pass and shoot like Pete. I quit being myself and tried to be somebody else.

If you have put an athlete on a pedestal, you are in a dangerous position. Eventually, that athlete will do something to let you down because the athlete is human. All people have sinned and fallen short of the glory of God. All people are imperfect and will eventually fall short and disappoint you. Pray that God will give you a proper perspective to enjoy the athlete's performance but never put the athlete on a pedestal or make the athlete a god in your life. The Bible teaches that placing people on pedestals is sinful because that's when you put them above God. Know where to draw the line. If you find yourself way down because an athlete or team lost, then you might have lost perspective. The ability to maintain proper perspective is one of the wonderful benefits of being a child of God. If you are a believer, the Holy Spirit will help you maintain balance and perspective the next time your favorite athlete does something great or throws a bad interception.

Prayer: Father God, thank you for what I can learn from great athletes and the ways that I can enjoy their performances. Help me realize that only you are to be placed on a pedestal, your throne. In Jesus's holy name, amen.

BK11:
THE MIRACLE IN THE
GEORGIA DOME

Hebrews 1:12, 13:8; James 1:17

But you are the same, and your years shall not fail.

Hebrews 1:12

I was in the Georgia Dome for the 2008 SEC Basketball Championship the night a tornado hit and witnessed the miracle shot only minutes before the building shook. At noon that day, in a pouring rainstorm, I scrounged three tickets downtown so that Becca, Allison, and I could see our beloved Kentucky Wildcats. The first game in the evening session was Alabama and Mississippi State. With one second remaining in regulation and Bama down by three, Mykal Riley hit a twenty-four-foot shot to send the game into overtime. But it was the way the ball went in the basket that earned the nickname "the miracle shot." The ball rattled around, hit the backboard, hit the front iron, teetered, and finally fell in. Last-second shots just don't do that. It was as if God tipped in the shot to send the game to OT.

Ten minutes later, the players on the court backed away from the north side of the court, staring at the ceiling as the tornado brushed the Georgia Dome. The sound was like the classic freight train. It appeared that giant animals were making paw prints all over the fabric roof of the dome. I stood transfixed, watching debris fall from the roof, as Becca and Allison yelled at me to move for safe cover.

There is universal agreement that Riley's shot saved many lives that evening. If Riley's shot didn't go in, hundreds of Alabama fans would have headed immediately for the exits to make the drive to Alabama. You don't hang around at tournaments when your team gets eliminated. That departure would have put them directly in the path of a 130-mile-per-hour twister, because there was no warning from Georgia Dome event management.

God is still in the miracle business because he never changes. Hebrews 13:8 tells us that Jesus Christ is the same yesterday, today, and forever. God speaks to people through modern-day miracles. God might use different approaches in the twenty-first century because there was no game called basketball two thousand years ago. So his ways change, but what will never change is his desire to see everyone come to know Jesus Christ. That's why he has been so patient, giving everyone an opportunity to know Jesus before he comes back. In heaven, I believe that the saints will know the impact of God's mercy on his kingdom through the Georgia Dome miracle, God's wake-up call to the twenty-five thousand in attendance that evening.

Prayer: Most gracious and merciful God, thank you for the modern-day miracles that affect lives for eternity. In Jesus's name, amen.

BK12:
PILGRIMAGE TO BATON ROUGE

John 14:6

I am the Way, the Truth, and the Life. No one comes to the Father except through Me.

On November 2, 2003, I dedicated my life to Jesus Christ at the age of forty-eight after watching a VHS tape of a testimony by Pete Maravich. I received God's free gift of grace and eternal life in heaven. Only six weekends prior, Becca, Allison, Jillian, and I traveled to Baton Rouge for the LSU-UGA football game. It was my first trip ever to Baton Rouge, and I was thrilled to walk inside the Cow Palace, also known as the John W. Parker Ag Center, and imagine what it was like to be in an overflow crowd watching Pete go for another fifty. Allison and I walked by Tiger Stadium to the Pete Maravich Assembly Center, named for Pete shortly after his death in 1988, and took some photos as some LSU fans razzed us. I knew Pete was in heaven and how he came to know Christ, but I was so into me that I rarely thought about my future and my eternity. It is still amazing to me how God used Pete's testimony on a VHS tape to bring me to Christ in my den only six weeks later.

Fast forward five years to October 2008, and it was time for Georgia to visit LSU again on the five-year SEC schedule rotation. I just had to go back. How different my life was then, but I still needed to grow so much. That summer, I became spiritually lazy and rested on my laurels after spearheading our first church golf tournament, Golf for His Glory. As I stood in my closet one afternoon, the thought hit me that Pete had died five years after becoming a Christian. Here I was approaching the fifth anniversary of being a Christian, and I hadn't done squat for Christ lately. It was a real wake-up call, and I prayed that my trip to Baton Rouge this time would honor God and be one of spiritual renewal.

On a picture-perfect Friday, I left Becca in New Orleans and drove to the LSU campus. I received a personal tour of the Maravich Center from the operations manager and thoroughly enjoyed seeing Pete's memorabilia in Pete Maravich Pass, dedicated to Pete's memory in 2007. I walked throughout the Cow Palace, even down in the bowels of what is now a rodeo facility. Finally, I went out to Resthaven Gardens in East Baton Rouge to pay homage to the man God used to bring me to Christ. I knelt at Pete's marker, read John 14 silently, talked to God, and gave God the glory for using Pete to save me. Later, I thought, *Who will one day visit my grave and thank me for leading them to Christ?*

Who will one day kneel at your grave and thank you? When we get to heaven, I believe one of the coolest things will be to see the amazing tapestry that God has woven as he has chosen to use flawed human beings to advance his kingdom. I believe we will get to see our spiritual tree and celebrate with those who came before us and will come after us.

Prayer: Heavenly Father, thank you for the Christian legacy of Peter Press Maravich and the events that you use in my daily life to draw me closer to you so that I can enjoy a life that is dedicated to the kingdom of God. In Jesus's name, amen.

BK13:
RECEIVING MERCY ...
FROM A REFEREE?

Lamentations 3:22–26, 32; Philippians 1:6

His mercies are new every morning...

Lamentations 3:23

When you are a new basketball player, it's difficult to learn and obey all of the rules. If the referee called every rules violation that players committed, the game would be 2–0 or 4–2. That game would not be much fun to play, nor would it be much fun to watch. The referee should always call violations such as running with the ball, three seconds, double dribble, and fouls when a clear advantage is gained illegally by a player. Hard, physical fouls need to be called to keep players safe and lessen the chance of injury. The referee actually shows you *mercy* by not penalizing you when you make mistakes as you learn to play the game and protects you from injury by controlling the physical play in the game.

You should be very thankful that God also shows you mercy when you are a new Christian. Even though you become a Christian, you still have many years before you become a mature Christian. God wants to encourage you, especially in your first few years. If God called you out on every sin and gave you the full measure that you deserve, you could become very discouraged and never get off the starting line. When we are baby Christians, God will correct us through the Holy Spirit but not discipline us as severely as he will years later. The longer that we have been Christians, the higher his expectations are for us to live a life that is perfect in Christ. So if you are a fairly new Christian, like a toddler, God will give you some cool surprises to encourage your walk and to keep you excited and motivated about growing as a Christian. Praise God that he knows exactly what each of us needs to grow in love and obedience.

Prayer: Father God, thank you for your mercy and compassion, and for not giving me the full measure of what I deserve when I break your rules. In Jesus's name, amen.

BK14:
THE GREATEST 360 IN HISTORY

Mark 15:25–37

It was the third hour, and they crucified him…at the ninth
hour Jesus cried with a loud voice…

Mark 15:25, 37

One of the most dramatic, athletic, and thrilling plays in basketball is a
breakaway 360 slam dunk. A 360 dunk means that the player leaves his
feet while facing the basket, goes high into the air, and rotates his body
a full 360 degrees or one complete revolution before slamming the ball
home. Many players have mastered this move, and fans will debate
which athlete has been the best at the 360. When I asked my players
at open gym one night about the greatest 360 dunk they had seen, one
young man named Jullian said without hesitation, "Vince Carter at the
All-Star game [Toronto, 2000]." Still others mentioned Kobe Bryant.
And from a generation ago, I told them about Dominique Wilkins,
the Atlanta Hawks star who was nicknamed the human highlight film
because of his spectacular dunks and aerial maneuvers. Whoever executes a 360 dunk causes the fans to go crazy and spill their popcorn
in celebration.

After I asked our players who the greatest 360 dunker was, I asked
them to tell me the greatest 360 in history—not just in basketball or
in sports, but in history. None of them followed me, so I read them

two verses from the book of Mark. The first verse said simply that Jesus Christ was crucified at nine in the morning. The second verse stated that the skies turned black from noon to 3:00 P.M., at which time Jesus declared, "It is finished," and gave up his spirit. Jesus hung on the cross for you and me from 9:00 A.M. to 3:00 P.M. Let's do the math. Six hours times sixty minutes per hour is *360 minutes*. The greatest 360 in history is because of what the cross and the demonstration of love meant for mankind. Jesus didn't just drink from the cup. He drained it and tasted every drop of sin that will ever be committed. As if to make a point, because prophetically he could have come down well before then, he hung and hung and hung to show Satan, "Who's your daddy now?" Jesus showed his amazing love for us by continuing to pull himself up to draw one more breath, raking his torn and bleeding back against the splinters on the cross for 360 minutes, the greatest 360 there ever was, is, and is to come.

Prayer: Dear Jesus Christ, what an incredible gift of love you gave me when you hung a 360 on the rugged cross for me. In Jesus's name, amen.

BK15:
THE NEXT TIME I SEE PISTOL

Philippians 1:20–21

For to me, to live is Christ, and to die is gain.

Philippians 1:21

I vividly recall the last time that I saw Pete Maravich, and it was the closest that I had ever physically been to him. The scene was the old Omni Arena in Atlanta in 1980. The Hawks had just defeated the Celtics on a last-second shot by Eddie Johnson. Pete had played sparingly in his backup role with the Celtics, and the biggest reaction that night had been to his new perm 'do and the rainbow layups he kissed off the glass during warm-ups. Even in a backup role, Pete enthralled his legion of fans.

After the game, my friend, Joel, and I went down to the dressing room to get another glimpse of Pete. I looked up and Pete was standing by the wall, talking to a group of admirers and friends. Joel pleaded, "Go on over there! Go meet him." Joel understood perhaps better than anyone my infatuation and idol worship of Pistol. I wanted so desperately to meet him, but I respected his privacy. And what if he rejected me? My biggest fear was that Pete wouldn't react to me like I wanted him to, me, his biggest fan who pressed his ear to a transistor radio and listened to him score sixty-eight against the Knicks and who was shattered when Pete blew out his knee and missed his All-Star homecoming in Atlanta.

I would never see Pistol again. He retired after that season. I met my future wife, Becca, that summer. Georgia won the national championship. We married, and Allison and Jillian were born in 1984 and 1987. I thought of him sparingly over the years and was vaguely aware that Pete had dedicated his life to Christ. On January 5, 1988, I walked in the door from work, and Joel was on the phone. "Did you hear about Pistol? He died of a heart attack in a pickup basketball game today." I said, "You're kidding me. That can't be." Joel said, "You know I wouldn't kid you about that." I was in a bit of shock. I began to reflect as the ESPN sportscast replayed a recent interview with Pete as Pete described the difference that Jesus Christ had made in his life. But it didn't cause me to reflect on my missing relationship with Christ. I had plenty going on with my job, my growing family, and a promising college refereeing career. Sure, I had kept my Pistol number 7 Jazz home jersey in my closet for the past ten years and would keep it for the next fifteen. But who could have known that fifteen years later, I would watch a video tape of Pete's testimony that would draw me to the Son?

And now, someday, I will see Pete again. When I enter the pearly gates, maybe he'll hit me with a behind-the-back pass for an easy layup. My dad and Pete's dad, Press, will be there to coach, and my mom will keep score just like she did when my dad coached. Pistol, I can't wait to see you again.

Prayer: Dear Lord, thank you for the legacy of Pistol Pete, which is still bringing people into the kingdom of God. In Jesus's name, amen.

BK16:
HOOPIN' IT UP IN COSTA RICA

Matthew 9:37–38, 28:19–20

Therefore, go and make disciples in all the nations …

Matthew 28:19

The summer after I was saved, I went with a Mt. Zion UMC mission team to Costa Rica. My former pastor, Tom Pilgrim, said that I should go to help me grow, so I went. The personal highlight of the trip was taking about seventy pounds of sports equipment to the Cartago church. In the suitcase were a makeshift wooden backboard, a basketball hoop and net, and some deflated basketballs. One afternoon, my friend, David, and I bolted the backboard and rim to a mahogany post in the dirt-laden church yard and we burned up three drill bits in the process. But once the goal was up there, it wasn't coming down. I figured it would last for two weeks, but two years later, a mission team brought me pictures of the hoop still standing.

As I had hoped, basketball turned out to be a great way to meet the kids from the neighborhood. I have some great pictures of American and Costa Rican kids playing five on five. The dirt court was so black that after minutes of handling the ball, your hands would be pitch black. I became friends with Daniel, Isaac, Kenneth, and the pastor's son, David (pronounced Da-veed). After we played for the final time on a Thursday afternoon, I shared my testimony with the boys and told them all about Pistol Pete Maravich through Eric, our interpreter. But I failed to offer them an opportunity to receive Christ. I still didn't realize that God had blessed me with a story that he could use to change lives. Once I realized that God had blessed me with this special gift, it haunted me for some time that I had not given them this opportunity. The missed opportunity helped me know how important it is to take advantage of chances to share Christ with others as the Holy Spirit leads.

Prayer: Most wonderful Father, give me the discernment and courage to pull the net for your kingdom when the Spirit leads. Give me a heart and a burden for the unsaved. In Jesus's name, amen.

BK17:
CAN YOU TRACE YOUR ROOTS IN CHRIST?

Acts 2:1–17, Exodus 20:4–6

I will pour out of my Spirit upon all flesh …

Acts 2:17

One evening, I read the story of Henrietta Mears, a wonderful Christian saint who began a Sunday school class in Southern California that reached thousands of people for Christ beginning in the 1930s. Mears started a summer camp in the San Bernardino Mountains for youth, and one young man who came through her camp in 1951 was Bill Bright, who would begin the Campus Crusade for Christ ministry. Bill Bright is given credit for millions of people receiving Christ during his fifty-year ministry through Campus Crusade and his production and distribution of *The Jesus Film.*

One young man who came through Bright's San Bernardino camp in the summer of 1966 was a six-foot-five-inch shooting guard named Pistol Pete Maravich. Perhaps someone sensed that Pete was about to throw away a promising college and pro career through his reckless life-style, because Pete received an invitation to put on his *Showtime* clinic at the event. To make a long story short, Pete drove over four thousand miles and never did a clinic. Instead, he was placed in a small group for three days. When Bright gave the invitation to receive Christ, Pete rejected Jesus and was quite cavalier and defiant about it.

But sixteen years later, when Pete was at his wit's end one night when all of the sins he had committed kept coming up in his mind, he remembered the seeds that had been sown at Bright's camp and the message of salvation. Pete received Christ in November 1982 at the foot of his bed at five thirty in the morning. Three years later, Pete would give a testimony in Phoenix, Arizona, that was taped and became a hot item after Pete died suddenly in 1988.

I bought the testimony tape in 2003 on eBay and was saved after watching it on November 2, 2003. It was a startling and cool revelation to see how Mears to Bright to Maravich to Farr had evolved. Apparently, others have received Christ through my testimony to FCA groups, youth groups, and the youth sports ministry.

I believe one day we will see this amazing believer-ology tree in heaven that will show us the Christian lineage of person after person, generation after generation. We will see the impact that we had on the lives of other believers.

How do you trace your Christian lineage? Was it your father, mother, youth pastor, friend, Sunday school teacher, or VBS volunteer? Perhaps it was a close friend whom you admired or an athlete, as was my case. Do you even have a lineage to trace? Generations of your family will be influenced by the choices you make for or against Christ.

Prayer: Most holy and powerful God, what confidence you had when you trusted twelve ordinary men to carry the torch of salvation after Jesus ascended. May I help continue the lineage that these brave disciples began. In Jesus's name, amen.

BK18 :
NEED A FRESH JERSEY?

2 Corinthians 5:17; John 11:25–26, 14:6; 1 John 1:9

The one who lives and believes in Me will never die—ever.
Do you believe this?

John 11:26

At our summer basketball camps and league play, some nights, the A/C doesn't work very well. The temperature in the gym can be eighty degrees, which means plenty of sweaty bodies. We use reversible jerseys to move kids between teams so that the games remain competitive. Those sweaty jerseys become stinky jerseys after a couple of nights, especially if the jerseys are thrown into a pile. The next day, if you pick one up and take a good sniff, you might need smelling salts to revive you. By hanging up the jersey and letting it air out, it's not so bad, but the stench is still there. The only way to get a fresh, clean-smelling jersey is to wash it in soapy water. The clean smell returns, and that jersey is worth wearing again. You exchange a stinky, smelly, foul-smelling jersey for a fresh, clean, sweet-smelling jersey.

Before we knew Christ, our life's odor to God was always like that stinky, smelly jersey in the pile for three days. The odor came from the buildup of sin in our lives because we consistently disobeyed his law, which angers God. Don't believe we stink before we are saved? It's true. The only way to get rid of our putrid odor is to be washed clean by the blood of the Lamb. We don't change our lives so much as we *exchange* our old lives for new lives in Christ. Paul made it clear in 2 Corinthians that when someone becomes a Christian, he or she becomes a new person. The old person is out; in with the new.

I heard Paige, a former missionary to the Russian republic of Kazakhstan, share this story that helps illustrate the point. One afternoon, she was on a bus in Kazakhstan, sitting across the aisle from a man whose odor she described as simply repulsive. He had open sores, his hair was dirty, his clothes were filthy, and his odor reeked across the aisle. As she looked at him, she sensed God speaking to her. *What? You don't think your sin is smelly, stinky, and repulsive to me?*

Just as we exchange a filthy jersey for a clean one, we exchange our filthy, sinful nature for one that is pure in Christ. When you turn from sin and place your trust in Christ, immediately you are cleansed by the blood of our precious Savior and given the Holy Spirit. As Jesus works within you, the difference in your new life versus your old life should become as striking as the difference between the putrid jersey and the clean jersey.

You will constantly get ugly stains (sin) on your new jersey. But the way to get rid of them is to spot clean your jersey. Tell God exactly what caused the spot and where the spot is, and together, Jesus and God will cleanse you. First John 1:9: "If we confess our sins, he is faithful and just, and will forgive our sins, and cleanse us from all unrighteousness."

You will stain your new jersey, but you should not retain the stench of your old jersey. If you do, you might be a false convert, having never actually received the Holy Spirit. A false convert hears the Word and gets excited for a while but falls by the wayside when trials and temptations come.

Go ahead and sniff your jersey. Need a fresh one? Jesus is holding a clean number 1 jersey just for you. Jesus said, "I am the Way, the Truth, and the Life." Jesus is the only way to God and to heaven.

Prayer: Father God, thank you for spot-cleaning me when I confess what I have messed up and for making me as pure as snow again. In Jesus's name, amen.

BK19:
THE FINALS

Matthew 7:21–29

I never knew you. Depart from me, you who practice lawlessness.

Matthew 7:23

The National Basketball Association calls its championship series The Finals, which pits the Eastern Conference champion against the Western Conference champion. Can you name the winner of the The Finals in 1999? How about 2004? If The Finals were truly final, then perhaps you and I could remember who the champion was. If The Finals were played this year and never played again, we would remember the champion.

The day of judgment is the finals when God returns the verdict on your life. You will either be a big winner or a big loser on that day. There won't be another day of judgment, a second chance or a replay. You will be the biggest winner ever if you repented of your sins and took Jesus as your Savior during this lifetime. When judgment day comes for you, Jesus will act as your intercessor. When you come face to face with God Almighty and are too awestruck to utter your name, Jesus will speak on your behalf and say: "Father, this is (Your Name). I know (Your Name). Remember that on (date), (Your Name) repented and accepted me as Savior. I paid the penalty for (Your Name's) sins on the cross. I bore those sins in my body on the cross. You remember, right?" When Jesus intercedes for you, God will welcome you to heaven with open and loving arms for all eternity. If you never made that commitment, Jesus will say, "I'm sorry. I never knew (Your Name)." The Bible promises that there will be weeping, torment, and gnashing of teeth for all eternity.

Prepare for these finals today by repenting of your sins and inviting Christ into your heart. The best time to plant a tree is today. The same goes for determining your salvation for eternity. Today is the best day.

Prayer: Father God, thank you for making Jesus my intercessor to represent me on judgment day. May he recognize me and speak for me, having paid the price for me on the cross for my sin. May I see you both in heaven. In Jesus's name, amen.

BK20:
BEATING THE ODDS

Luke 12:40

So be ready at all times, for I, the Messiah, will come when least expected.

If you coach a basketball team, pick your best shooter to shoot a series of shots at practice. Before the player shoots, ask the players how many believe that the player will make a layup. Most, if not all, hands will go up. Have the player shoot the layup. Then repeat the procedure for a ten-footer, a free throw, a three-pointer, a half-court shot, and a seventy-foot desperation heave. Note that fewer hands go up with each shot. I doubt any player will raise his hand seriously for the seventy-footer.

Explain to the players that the odds of receiving Christ are similar to making those shots. The odds of coming to know Christ is much greater in grade school (like the layup and ten-footer), but the odds become increasingly longer in middle school (the free throw), high school (the three-pointer), college (thirty-footer), and adulthood (the half-court or desperation shot).

By the time a person reaches forty to fifty years of age and is not a believer, experts have estimated that less than 10 percent, or one in ten, will become a believer. As unconfessed sin builds up, it hardens your heart like rings on a tree. You become less receptive to the Word and more skilled in your ability to fool yourself, especially if you are leading a successful, comfortable life that appears to reflect your success.

Why would you want to mess with good when so many other people around you have it bad? By the way, the odds of making the seventy-foot desperation heave are about the same as a deathbed conversion, probably less than 1 percent. Please don't allow time to run out when eternity is at stake.

The odds are certain that some players on your team or members of your family will never go to heaven. Beat the odds personally by surrendering your life to Christ while you're young. The sooner the better, before the odds become stacked against you.

Prayer: Father God, may I be perfectly in tune with your will and your plan for my life, which includes being in heaven with you one day. Help me understand that the longer I wait the greater the risk that I will be eternally separated from you. In Jesus's name, amen.

BK21:
PISTOL PETE'S BOX SCORE
(PART 1)

Hebrews 10:17, Romans 12:1–2, John 14:6

Do not be conformed, but be transformed by the renewing of your mind...

Romans 12:2

On February 25, 1977, Pete Maravich scored sixty-eight points on twenty-six field goals and sixteen free throws against the New York Knicks, even though he fouled out with a minute to play. As he left the floor, eleven thousand fans chanted, "Pete! Pete! Pete!" But Pete was a restless, discontented person off the court and showed little joy on the court. He shared that he didn't want to get up the next morning because people would expect sixty-eight again. Sure enough, a CBS TV announcer issued this challenge before his next game: "Pete can prove he is really this good if he scores forty today." Note: Pete had thirty-five at the half and finished with forty-three.

Pistol Pete's Basketball Box Score

Name	FG	FG Attempts	FT	FT Attempts	Assists	Rebounds	Total Score
Maravich	26	43	16	19	5	6	68

But Pete's life box score did not resemble his basketball box score. Pete was not a Christian when he scored sixty-eight. He did not have a relationship with Jesus Christ, although he went to church as a child. When he was a teenager, Pete rejected Christ at a Campus Crusade event in California. Pete thought being a Christian would interfere with his worldly basketball goals. He was defiant and said that Jesus Christ on the cross was "just a story." Pete thought that he was a pretty good guy, that he could do as he pleased so long as he didn't hurt anybody. Although he had a great family with two sons and was a millionaire when a million was a lot of money, he was miserable until Christ became his Savior and Lord.

Your daily box score without Christ could look like this on a typical day.

Helped Poor	Witnessed	Read Bible	Prayed	Meditated	Worshipped	Helped Family	Fellowship
0	0	0	0	0	0	1	0

Prayer: Father God, help me to see where I am making turnovers in my life. Thank you that you encourage me to tell you when I've messed up. You already know anyway, and I thank you that you will always forgive and forget when I sincerely confess my mistakes. In Jesus's name, amen.

BK22:
PISTOL PETE'S BOX SCORE
(PART 2)

Romans 12:2, Colossians 3:17

So that you may prove what is that good and acceptable and perfect will of God.

Romans 12:2

Pete experienced a dramatic transformation in Christ, as evidenced by his deeds and actions. One Thanksgiving, Pete bought a hundred turkeys, and he and his pastor delivered them to the poor families in Baton Rouge. Pete witnessed throughout the United States, and God used him to bring hundreds of people to know Jesus Christ through these talks and his Christian basketball camp in Florida. Pete studied the Bible for hours at a time and became well-versed in Scripture. Bible study and prayer were key to Pete's rapid growth and transformation as a Christian because he trained and renewed his mind each day. Del Wubbena, who helped Pete start his Christian basketball camp, once told me, "Pete grew more in five years than any man I have ever known." Pete led his wife and dad to accept Christ. He cared for his dad night and day for six months before Press died of cancer. Pete developed strong relationships with other brothers in Christ. He donated speaking engagement money to nonprofit charities and his church.

Sure, Pete had his weak moments and fell down like we all do. After his conversion, Pete drank a few beers one day, and the next day, he poured the wine from his expensive collection down the kitchen sink. He apologized to people he had hated or he had hurt, even though the circumstances that separated them had happened many years ago. This story is not simply to tell you what a great guy Pete Maravich became. It is to illustrate the greatness of God and Jesus Christ, and turning to Jesus is how amazing transformations begin for Pete, for me, and for you. Your daily box score in Christ could look like these.

Good Deeds in the Name of Christ Box Score

Helped Poor	Witnessed	Read Bible	Prayed	Meditated	Worshipped	Helped Family	Fellow-ship
3	4	2`	5	1	1	4	3

Reflect briefly on what your box score looks like so far today. Are your good deeds outweighing the bad ones? The good news is that we are all works in progress. As you grow in Christ, you will become less conscious of your good deeds because they will just evolve naturally from your relationship with Christ. That's what happened to Pistol Pete, and it can happen for you!

Prayer: Dear Father, thank you for what I can learn from the legacy of Pete Maravich, a man who dedicated himself to sharing the gospel with so many people. May I emulate his example of witnessing for you whenever I get the chance. In Jesus's name, amen.

BK23:
BE READY TO COME OFF THE BENCH

Hebrews 12:1, Luke 12:40

Throw off everything that so easily entangles us ...

Hebrews 12:1

Many times, when the outcome of a game hangs in the balance, the decisive play is not made by the MVP, or the leading rebounder, or even a starter, but by a substitute who comes off the bench. In basketball, there are twelve to fifteen players on a team, but only five can start the game. It's really important that the non-starters pay close attention, study the game, and be ready at all times. You might suddenly be rushed into the game if a player is injured. You might only have a brief opportunity to help the team, and you want to make the most of that chance. If you aren't ready, you won't make the play that your team needs.

As a Christian, sometimes you feel as if you are not in the game for God. Either you've not studied his Word or haven't been in prayer with him lately. Perhaps there is a secret sin that has derailed you temporarily. When the opportunity comes to listen to a friend who needs to vent, or to share Christ when someone opens a door, you miss it like a breakaway layup ahead of the field. The biggest detriment is our attitude, which can be self-centered, especially when sin has separated us from God. Just like a player rips off his warm-ups to enter the game, you must be prepared to "throw off everything (sin) that easily entangles (you)," so you can "run with perseverance the race set before (you)."

If you focus on loving God and all the daily blessings he gives you and especially remember the sacrifice that Christ made on the cross for you, then you will want to return his love and be obedient. If you are obedient, you will stay ready and see where God is working. That is where the opportunities to help grow God's kingdom are. Even as insignificant as you might feel, your contributions could make the difference for a friend or family member for eternity. Remember, God chose to operate with twelve very ordinary, challenging, and disparate individuals who changed the world after they received the Holy Spirit. After you have received the Holy Spirit, you are no different from Andrew and Peter. Trust that God can do a mighty work through you, even when you feel like a part-time player.

Prayer: Dear Lord, help me stay true to you so that I'm ready to leap off the bench to make a play for the kingdom of God. In Jesus's name, amen.

BK24:
DO NOT FEAR

Deuteronomy 31:6, Joshua 1:9, Hebrews 13:5

I will never leave you nor forsake you.

Hebrews 13:5

Since my father was a high school coach, and my mother was the score-keeper, and my older sister, Regina, and older brother, L. E., were out-standing basketball players, I have been in gyms since I was in diapers. I was a gym rat, no question. I have been to state tournaments with Dad's teams and always sat on the bench with him. I have been in big crowds at Atlanta Braves games and was around exciting sports events all of my life. But when I was thirteen and fourteen, panic attacks seized me at ball games. I can remember playing in a region tourna-ment game when I was a sophomore. I was barely five feet tall, and when our guards fouled out, Coach Lake had no choice but to play me. I was so nervous that I was fighting for my breath, and I was prob-ably hyperventilating. Somehow, I managed to get through the game. In fact, I stole a pass in overtime that helped us win the game. A local sportswriter described the steal as having been made by "Danny Farr, at four feet eleven inches, the smallest high school player in the state of Georgia." Man was I embarrassed. A similar anxiety attack had hap-pened at the boys' first round game at state the previous year and at the girls' state tournament. There was no reason for it. Eventually, the bad feelings passed, and I haven't had a problem since.

Those episodes made me reflect on why I was fearful. I had nothing to fear. How much better off I would have been if I had gone to God and asked him to help me? But Christ was not part of my life, even though I had that great opportunity to receive him as my Savior when I was thirteen. The Bible tells us 365 times not to fear, once for each day of the year. "Do not be afraid . . . for the Lord your God is with you wherever you go" (Joshua 1:9). All you need to do is "draw near to God, and God will draw near to you" (James 4:8) and protect you. How I wish that I had realized back then that the Lord my God was with me wherever I went to guide me and protect me. He will take you through your difficult situations if you let him. As a believer, I have no reason to fear man, and no matter what happens on this earth, my eternity in heaven is assured. What a comforting thought for Christians.

Prayer: Dear Lord God Almighty, when I am fearful, please remind me that you are there to lead me, guide me, hold me, and protect me from harm. In Jesus's holy name, amen.

BK25:
THE NAIL AT THE
FREE-THROW LINE

Luke 23:32–34, Isaiah 53:1–5, Psalm 22:16

By His stripes we are healed.

Isaiah 53:5

On many basketball courts, a single nail is driven at each end of the court to mark the exact center of the free-throw line. That spot is exactly six feet from either side of the free-throw lane line. When a player shoots a free throw, a player carefully aligns at a perfect 90-degree angle with the front of the rim. The shooter ensures that the forearm is exactly perpendicular to the basket so that the odds of making the shot are the greatest. The release and follow through should point directly toward the front of the rim. The greater the angle the tougher the shot. When the player places one foot directly behind the nail, the player *knows* that he or she is centered perfectly, and the player's confidence level increases.

You and I need to be perfectly aligned with Christ and place him at the exact center of our lives. You center Christ in your life when all aspects of your life are under his guidance. Remember that Christ took the nails for you and me so that we could be freed from the control of sin in our lives and we could choose to receive the free gift of eternal life in heaven. Remember how Jesus took a nail through his feet that was driven into the wooden cross? He was pierced for your sin and mine. To be Christ-centered, you must truly turn from all of your sins, place your trust in Jesus, obey him daily by reading the Word, being in prayer, and truly worship God.

The next time you shoot a free throw, look down to see if someone drove a nail into the wood for you so that you could find the center of the free throw line. Let that nail remind you to stay Christ-centered on and off the court.

Prayer: Dear Father God, when I use my hands and feet today, I will give thanks that Jesus took the nails in his hands and feet for me so that I could be free to live from the clutches of sin. Help me stay centered in Christ today. In Jesus's name, amen.

BK26:
FIX YOUR EYES ON THE TARGET

Hebrews 12:2

Looking unto Jesus, the author and perfector of our faith …

I asked a group of basketball campers where they aim when they shoot. The replies came back quickly: "The basket," "The backboard." The backboard? Why not just aim at the back wall. Their aims weren't specific at all. I explained that it is very important for a shooter to pick a specific point at which to aim. When I shoot a free throw, I pick out the eyelet (the hook that holds the net strand) on the very front of the rim. Then I try to drop the ball over the eyelet into the basket. The eyelet gives me a very specific aim point.

If you shoot an arrow at a target, do you aim at the entire circle or at the bull's eye? If you want a car or your bicycle to go straight, you pick out a spot in the distance and the car or bike just seems to go to that spot. Take your eye off the spot, and the car or bike drifts left or right.

That's how it is with maintaining focus in your life. If you look here and then over there and then somewhere else for answers and for direction, you'll be all over the map. Hebrews 12:2 teaches us to keep our eyes on Jesus, who is the author (Creator) and perfector of our faith. If you stay focused daily on Jesus, you won't be wandering here and there, searching for answers. Jesus is the only answer to the most important question that matters. How do I get to heaven? If you stay focused on Jesus and seek his guidance, you will eventually discern the unique plan that God has made for you. A key ingredient of the plan is your inborn passion. Everybody has a passion for something. The key is finding it and then channeling that passion for Christ. You don't know how? Keep your eye on Jesus and the Holy Spirit living within you, and God will do the rest. When you look at Jesus, you can know that your future is safe.

Keep your eye on the eyelet of the rim, and keep your eyes on Jesus, who endured the cross and scorned its shame just for you.

Prayer: Dear Father God, help me stay focused each and every hour of each and every day on Jesus. When I fall short, please forgive me. In Jesus's holy and precious name, amen.

BK27:
DON'T BECOME DISTRACTED

Luke 9:62

Anyone who allows himself to be distracted from the work that I plan for him is not fit for the Kingdom of God.

As a boy, Pistol Pete Maravich practiced basketball eight to ten hours a day in the summer in sweltering, empty gyms. One summer day, he began to cry while sitting in the floor of the Clemson College gym, wondering what possibly drove him to such lengths when his friends were at the lake. *Why am I here? Why do I have this desire? Why am I killing myself?* he wondered. But he got up and resumed one of the forty or fifty ball-handling drills his father and coach, Press, had created for him. Pete wasn't about to give up his three goals of earning a college scholarship, making a million dollars, and being a world champion. God made Pete to be able to concentrate on repetitive tasks for long periods of time. As Pete mastered the fundamental skills, Press gave him more complicated drills, which Pete also mastered. He became so good at the drills that incredible passes, shots, and dribbles became routine. Even though Pete last played in the NBA in 1980, many experts still consider Pete to be the greatest ball handler, dribbler, and passer to ever play basketball.

Two years after he retired from professional basketball, Pete received Christ as his Savior and Lord. He approached his study of the Bible with the same type of fervor and dedication that rivaled his attention to basketball drills as a child. Pete stayed focused and did not allow himself to be distracted from daily Bible study and prayer.

It is very important as a Christian that you do not allow yourself to be distracted from your daily discipline of prayer and Bible reading. The fundamentals of prayer and Bible reading and the ability to apply those principles to complex daily activities allow God to use you for bigger responsibilities in his kingdom. If you allow yourself to get distracted, then you will drift away from God's plan, and his plan is always better than anything you and I can create.

Pete discovered God's plan for his life. He grew in his love for Christ and learned how to be obedient to God. As he learned, he kept his hand on the plow and sowed many seeds for God's kingdom that fell on fertile soil.

Prayer: Dear Father God, may I grow in my love for you and be obedient daily so that I can be about doing the work you have planned for me. In Jesus's name, amen.

BK28:
WHAT IS WORTH ETERNAL LIFE?

Ecclesiastes 2:11

Yet when I surveyed all that my hands have made, and what
I have toiled to achieve, everything is meaningless; a chasing
after the wind, nothing is gained under the sun.

Solomon penned this very poignant verse in the book of Ecclesiastes,
verse 2:11: "No matter what my hands have made, and what I have
toiled to achieve, everything is meaningless; a chasing after the wind,
nothing is gained under the sun."

Thirty-five-year-old Pete Maravich was a millionaire, a successful
gardener, investor, husband, father, and had been one of the great basketball players of all time. But he was miserable. When I break down
the verse from Ecclesiastes 2:11, it sums up Pete's life.

"Yet when I surveyed all that my hands have made." Pete was perhaps the greatest ball handler and had one of the best pair of hands in
the history of basketball. His legendary tricks and passes have thrilled
fans everywhere.

"And what I have toiled to achieve." Pete once told legendary
coach Red Auerbach, "You don't get this good by wishing." Pete spent
thousands of sweat equity hours perfecting his ball-handling skills to
become a great player.

"Everything is meaningless." Pete enjoyed immense fame and fortune that few people will ever achieve, but the whole experience left him empty. His life had no purpose.

"A chasing after the wind." Pete once drove his Porsche 130 miles per hour along the banks of Lake Pontchartrain in Louisiana and thought about turning his steering wheel ten degrees to the right, driving into the lake, and ending it all because he was so miserable. Pete had set fifty or sixty scoring records, but none of them made his team a champion.

"Nothing is gained under the sun." Pete never achieved the most important goal that his dad told him would make him a winner. That goal was the world championship ring. Pete bitterly left the Celtics in training camp during the season that Boston won the title in 1981.

But there was a joyous ending to Pete's story. In desperation one evening, Pete knelt by the side of his bed at five thirty in the morning and received Christ. The Holy Spirit came into Pete's heart, and Pete lived a full life for Christ during the last five years of his life.

Pete used his hands again to make the Pistol Pete Homework Basketball videos that millions have enjoyed since 1987. Pete toiled twelve-hour days to make the videos in the summer in a hot Louisiana gymnasium. This endeavor had meaning because Pete passed along his basketball artistry less than six months before he died in a gym in Pasadena, California. Pete stopped chasing the wind and seeking worldly pleasure under the sun and instead found the joy that he had missed for the first thirty-five years of his life.

Prayer: Father God, you certainly work in mysterious and creative ways. Thank you for what can be learned from the wonderful legacy of Pistol Pete. In Jesus's holy name, amen.

BK29:
AND ONE!

Romans 8:26

The Holy Spirit prays for us with such passion that it cannot be described in words.

The saying, "And one!" is very popular among basketball fans. Every fan thrills to see the old-fashioned three-point play when a flashy guard takes the ball to the basket, gets hit as he goes up, and twists his body to spin the ball off the glass into the basket. The fans leap to their feet, high-five each other, and scream, "And one!" *And one* means that the basket counts, and the player receives a free throw to convert the three-point play. In addition to the two-point basket, the player receives a bonus as a reward for the excellent play.

When you confess to God for the first time that you truly desire to turn away from your sinful life, God will grant you forgiveness because Jesus paid the penalty for your sin when he died on the cross. When you then place your trust in Jesus as your Savior, you receive God's free gift of grace and eternal life in heaven. You also receive an "and one" bonus because the same Holy Spirit that descended upon Jesus like a dove, and the same Holy Spirit that Jesus promised the disciples as a Comforter and Helper, takes up residence inside you as a person.

Hard to understand? Don't try to figure it out; just trust it. From the moment you receive Christ, the Holy Spirit takes up residence inside you to help with your daily problems. Concerned because you don't know how to pray or what to pray for? The Holy Spirit fills the gaps with such passion that I can't describe it here. In fact, it can't be described anywhere. It's so awesome. Remember repentance, forgiveness, and eternal life in heaven is through trust in Jesus Christ. And One, the Holy Spirit, will be with you forever.

Prayer: Father God, you are so good to me. Thank you for your blessings each day, and thank you for sending the Holy Spirit to live inside of me and guide me for the rest of my days. In Jesus's name, amen.

BK30:
DO YOU *KNOW* JESUS, OR DO YOU *THINK* YOU KNOW JESUS?

Matthew 7:23

I never knew you.

Ralph Sampson was a seven-feet-four-inches-tall basketball star and three-time collegiate All-American at the University of Virginia from 1980–1983 and played in the NBA for the Houston Rockets. He could dribble the ball behind his back and run the fast break like a guard, a truly astounding talent.

I heard this story about him from a former referee, who was an instructor at a basketball referee camp that I attended one summer at Robert Morris College in Pittsburgh. The storyteller was Dan Wooldridge, a long-time Atlantic Coast Conference referee. One night in Charlottesville, Dan made a questionable foul call against Ralph. The UVA fans went ballistic, which they tend to do when you assess a phantom foul against the most important player in a big ACC game. Ralph raised both arms high in the air, assuring his fans that he didn't touch his opponent. Wooldridge walked into the lane, looked up at Ralph, and said, "Ralph, I think you got him on the elbow," tapping his elbow to signify where he thought the contact happened. Ralph frowned and said, "Mr. Wooldridge, don't think it's a foul. Know it's a foul!" In other words, *know* that you have a foul before you call one.

Several years ago, Ralph was at Lassiter High School to watch his son play basketball. I introduced myself, recounted the story, and asked him if it was true. He nodded and said that was pretty much what had happened. He quickly added that Dan Wooldridge was a good guy.

Do you *know* that you are going to heaven, or do you think you are going? There is as big a difference between thinking and knowing as there is between black and white. If you think you know Jesus, you probably don't. For years, I occasionally wondered if my good works with the church basketball program would get me into heaven. But the night I heard Pete Maravich tell how Christ had transformed him, I could see it clearly. Pete quoted Jesus from Matthew 7:23, "I never knew *you*. Depart from me you who practice lawlessness." I knew that Jesus knew Pete, and I *knew* that Christ did *not know* me. I desperately vowed in my heart that I wanted my life to change, and it was at that moment that Jesus Christ knew me.

I never knew you. Because they came from Jesus, those are four of the saddest words in the Bible. I pray that you will come face to face with the realization that Christ either knows you or doesn't and that you know that your name is in the Book of Life or it isn't. If you aren't sure, remove any doubt by turning from your sinful ways and inviting Christ to come into your life.

Prayer: Father God, thank you for your divine Word that teaches me what I need to do to go to heaven when I die. Lead me, Holy Spirit, so that I will confess my sins and that Jesus will know me. In Jesus's name, amen.

BK31:
MASTER THE FUNDAMENTALS

Exodus 20:1–17, Joshua 1:8, Galatians 3:24

Wherefore the Law was our schoolmaster to bring us unto Christ ...

Galatians 3:24

Pete Maravich was arguably the greatest ball handler, dribbler, and passer the game has ever seen. Pete's repertoire of trick passes, fancy dribbles, and ball-handling drills are unparalleled even today. The Pistol put fans on the edge of their seats when he would cross half-court on a three-on-two fast break because they might see a pass they had never seen. Once an official called a travel on Pete for a slap pass, where Pete waves his hand over the ball and slaps it to a teammate. Pete questioned him, "How can you call that? You've never seen that move."

But Pete learned those amazing moves by building up to them. When he was a kid, his father and coach, Press Maravich, taught him the fundamentals of dribbling and passing. Dribble with the right hand, now with the left, alternate left and right. Execute the bounce pass, the chest bounce pass, and the baseball pass. Later came between-the-legs, behind-the-back, around-the-neck, and over-the-shoulder passes. Once Pete mastered the basics, he moved onto the advanced skills.

In a similar fashion, a person needs to master the fundamentals of the law in the form of the Ten Commandments. Every person is a born sinner, but first, one must learn the Ten Commandments to recognize sin. When you commit a sin and know that you broke one or more of the rules, you will realize that you need to repent and ask for God's forgiveness.

Too many people essentially want to throw the behind-the-back pass without learning the chest pass. They want the saving grace of the gospel before executing the fundamental of repentance. When they don't lead with repentance, they wonder years later why God failed them.

"Well, I gave my heart to Christ that night. Why am I still doing the same old same old?" First comes knowledge of the law and the realization of sinfulness that violates that law. Then comes a verdict of the lawlessness by the Holy Spirit, leading to godly sorrow, repentance, and then salvation through the cleansing blood of the Lamb.

Remember repentance first, then place your trust in Christ. Repentance won't save you, but you can't be saved without it. Who said it? Peter Press Maravich said it several years after accepting Christ as his Savior and Lord.

Prayer: Father God, I get confused sometimes and wonder what comes first. Help me always to know and share that repentance comes before accepting Christ. In the name of Jesus, who shed his blood at Calvary to cover my sins, amen.

BK32:
CEDAR GROVE GYM

Galatians 3:24, 1 John 1:7

If we walk in the Light as He is in the Light, we have
fellowship with one another, and the blood of Jesus Christ
cleanses us from all sin.

1 John 1:7

Dad was ninety-five years old when my brother, L. E., and I convinced
him to ride fifteen miles to Cedar Grove one Sunday morning after
church to see the gym where he coached his state championship team
in 1951. Dad had his best basketball teams in the 1950s in that gym.
The Cedar Grove community had preserved the exterior with tin sid-
ing, but the gym had been locked and boarded up for years. I desperately wanted to see inside the gym one more time. It had been the early
1970s since I had been inside when it was used as a community skating
rink. As a teenager I didn't appreciate the memories, not all of which
were pleasant. When I was four, I fell down the bleachers and busted
my mouth. I remember Mom holding a cup full of ice to my face before she had to keep score of the basketball game for Dad.

I walked behind the hallowed gym amid broken glass, weeds, and
underbrush. I saw a three-foot square opening in the back wall about
twelve feet above the ground because a fan had been removed. I managed to climb up rusty scaffolding and on my tiptoes I could see inside.

There it was. I can't describe the thrill to look inside and see the court. The backboards were gone, but the solid oak planks in the floor were still in good shape. I could faintly make out the baseline. Folding chairs were scattered about the far end of the gym. Most of the bleachers were still in place on the left side.

The reason that I could see at all was because there was a hole in the tin roof on the left side. The sunlight peered through the opening and lit the gym floor like a spotlight. Dust particles danced in the sunbeam as if part of a stream. What a thrill that I will always remember.

When God shines his Light upon us, it enables us to see our flaws in spite of our darkness. We can see the sin that we need to confess to God. Without the Light, we would continue to live in darkness. We need the contrast of good to highlight the evil. Without God's rules to correct us, we have no hope of shining his Light for the world to see how a Christian is supposed to live. We need the bright Light to reveal all of the sinful crevices in our hearts that can only be cleansed with the powerful cleansing blood of Jesus Christ.

I had wanted to see the inside of that gym for many years. When I finally saw it, it wasn't exactly what I expected. But it was such a thrill to rekindle fond memories that it felt like a little slice of heaven. Surely our reward will be so much greater when we see Jesus, the True Light, face to face one day.

Prayer: Thank you, Father God, for the special moments when we feel your presence and get a sense of what it will be like one day to come face to face in your holy presence. Until that time, may I live under the Light and allow the Light to show me where I need to be cleansed. In Jesus's holy name, amen.

BK33:
RULEBOOK OFFICIAL

Acts 26:4–5

...according to the strictest sect of our religion I lived a Pharisee.

Acts 26:5

I officiated college basketball for fifteen years and called about four hundred games at various levels, including a handful of Division 1 games. But first I refereed high school games. Each year, I had to pass a rules test or attend a rules clinic to certify that I understood the rules of basketball. Not only did I need to know the rules, but I needed to know how to interpret the spirit and intent of the rules. Once I understood the intent of the rules, I had to be able to apply the interpretation successfully. To be a successful college official, I had to apply the rules according to the level of play. There are certain calls in college that will put you back into high school officiating quicker than you can say, "The principle of verticality."

It is not enough to know the rules. Some officials make 100 on the rules test each year but can't referee their way out of a wet paper bag. They don't understand the application of the rule at the level of basketball that they are officiating. These officials are known in the trade as "rule book officials," who call every ticky tack foul that happens and ruin the flow of the game. The most successful officials know the rules, interpret them correctly, and apply them to achieve a fairly called, consistently officiated game.

The Bible and God's law require us to know the rules (e.g., Ten Commandments), to be able to interpret the rules, *and* to apply them to our daily lives. Those persons who are able to follow the rules consistently, who love and obey God, and who know Jesus Christ will eventually achieve real success. Not success as the world defines it in terms of money, power, and fame but blessings such as joy, peace, and riches that are far beyond monetary gain. What would some famous athletes and entertainers give for peace at this point in their lives?

If we aren't careful, we can be like the rulebook official. If we become so legalistic in our interpretation of the Bible but fail to live out its principles of love, mercy, grace, and forgiveness, we miss the forest for the trees. When Saul was a member of the Pharisee sect, he tried to keep from breaking over six hundred rules each day. He even wore a box that contained the rules on his sleeve to remind him. The end result was that he had plenty of head knowledge but didn't have any heart knowledge until his encounter with Christ on the road to Damascus. This heart knowledge is the ability to apply the teachings and produce the fruit of the Spirit, which enriches the lives of others in the name of Jesus Christ.

Prayer: Father God, may I understand the rules in the Bible so that I will understand when I break them. Restore me, oh God, so that I can live in full fellowship with you and be able to apply my learning so that I can enjoy the prosperity and success that comes only from knowing you and your holy Word. In Jesus's name, amen.

FOOTBALL

FB01:
THE BLIND SIDE REVISITED

Matthew 25:40, Mark 12:30–31, John 15:12, 1 John 3:17

This is my commandment. That you love one another, as I have loved you.

John 15:12

Becca and I saw a tremendous secular sports movie that also made a strong statement for Christ: *The Blind Side*. It stars Oscar-winner Sandra Bullock, who portrays Leigh Anne Tuohy, the wife of Sean Tuohy, a former Ole Miss basketball star. Leigh Anne's character is the perfect blend of Southern beauty, charm, street smarts, toughness, and compassion. *The Blind Side* is the true story of Michael Oher, a young man who was abandoned at birth by his father and at age seven by his mother in the toughest drug-infested section of Memphis. Michael gets a chance to attend a prestigious Christian school because of his size and athletic potential. Michael is eventually befriended and adopted by the Tuohys and becomes an All-American tackle at Ole Miss and a first-round draft choice of the Baltimore Ravens.

There are many poignant, heartwarming, compassionate scenes, but none more so than when Leigh Anne and Sean see him for the first time. Their son, S. J., and daughter, Collins, recognize him from school, and S. J. says, "That's Big Mike!" Big Mike is walking down the street in freezing weather in shorts and a tattered golf shirt. Leigh

Anne tells Sean to roll down the window of their luxury SUV, and she asks him if he needs a ride home. He assures them that he is fine, and they drive past him.

That's where the leading of the Holy Spirit kicks in. You can sense Leigh Anne's struggle as her brain processes the facts: *Cold night, no car, no jacket, by himself…What will happen if I help this very large African American boy?* Suddenly, Leigh Anne shouts to Sean, "Turn around!" Sean makes a U-turn, and they pick up Michael, take him to their home, and let him sleep overnight on the downstairs sofa.

Leigh Anne wore a beautiful diamond cross necklace throughout the movie. But that cross wouldn't have meant much if she had ignored the calling of the Holy Spirit to help this boy in need. Too often, I have an opportunity to help someone in need but ask, *How will this impact me?* Often, I commit a sin when I pass by putting my selfish needs ahead of others and the calling of Christ to help those in need. When I put my comfort ahead of others, I display my blind side to the world. My light doesn't shine for others to see his love. When Leigh Anne turned that car around, her Christian love shone brighter than her diamond cross.

Later in the movie, a friend remarks to Leigh Anne about how much Michael has changed. Actually, it is his circumstances that changed because Michael has a home, a family, three square meals a day, clothes on his back, and a great chance to earn a college scholarship. But he is still the same sweet Michael. Leigh Anne firmly replies, "He has changed me." When we reach out to others in the name of Christ, we find ourselves changed to be more like Christ.

Take your Kleenex and get ready to laugh and cry. Enjoy the movie and tell your friends, because you will all receive a blessing.

Prayer: Father God, I praise you for the courage of the Tuohys, the movie producers, and the directors who gave you honor and glory through this portrait of Christian love. I pray that you will use this movie to advance the cause of God's kingdom and motivate Christians everywhere to reach out in the name of Christ to brothers and sisters in need. In Jesus's name, amen.

FB02:
DISCOVER YOUR STASH

1 Chronicles 4:9–10; Matthew 7:7; John 10:10

Ask, and you will receive…

Matthew 7:7

When I was a kid, the local Coca-Cola bottler sponsored a giveaway, placing pictures of NFL players on the inside of bottle caps. There was nothing but bottles in those days, so that meant that a lot of caps were out there. My mother taught first grade and was great friends with the principal, so I could get all the bottle caps I wanted. About twice a week, Mom would get Mrs. Bedingfield to open the drink box so that I could empty the bottle caps from the container and take them home. That container of bottle caps was like a gold mine. I spent hours sorting through the caps and pasting them to sheets that contained room for fifty or sixty different caps. I filled twenty-three sheets when I only needed five sheets for a helmet or football. When Mom and I took twenty-three sheets to the Dublin Coca-Cola bottler, the Coca-Cola employee was stunned. At first, she only wanted to give me one prize, but Mom had my back. She knew that she and I had put a lot of effort into filling up those sheets. I think I walked away with one helmet and three "official" NFL footballs.

The spiritual message of this story is that when you have special connections in life, you can get some things that you normally wouldn't get. If I had to rely on only two or three bottle caps per day, I would have never filled up those sheets. In life, we come to God with only one or two blessings in mind. He wants to give us so much more if we will only ask. I am weak in this area, and I need to push the envelope more often because I know God wants to give me the very best.

From his abundant love, God wants to give us the entire bottle cap collection of blessings. In 1 Chronicles there is a great example of God's abundant blessing. There was a man named Jabez, who was more honorable than his brothers. Jabez offered a prayer to God asking him to "…bless me indeed, and enlarge my territory, that your Hand would be with me, and that you would keep me from evil, that I may not cause pain!" (1 Chronicles 4:10). When Jabez added the word indeed, he asked God for blessings that would be overflowing, and he received tremendous blessings from God.

God sent Jesus to us so that we could not only enjoy life but enjoy it abundantly. But we need to live for God through love and obedience, and then we just need to ask him like Mom asked Mrs. Bedingfield for the stash of bottle caps. God wants us to ask, seek, and knock so that we can receive the riches of his blessings, including the eternal gifts of salvation, joy, peace, and love. Let God shower you with a plethora of blessings each day. When you know Christ, you become eligible for the supernatural benefits of eternal life now and forevermore.

Prayer: Dear Father God, thank you for the bountiful abundance that you want to give me each day. Help me know that you want me to have so much more than I'm asking for. May I stay in loving obedience to you so that when I ask, I will receive. When I seek, I will find. When I knock, the door will be opened. In Jesus's name, amen.

FB03:
FIRST AND TEN

Exodus 20:1–17, 1 John 1:7

You shall have no other gods before me.

Exodus 20:3

Hearing that your favorite team has a first and ten is a welcome relief when your team has the football. Assuming there is enough time on the clock, your team has at least three plays and maybe four to make another first down, keep the drive alive, and go into the end zone for a touchdown. First and ten! Do it again!

Another first and ten known as the Ten Commandments must be *first* in our lives if we want to walk in the Light as he (Christ) is the Light. The *Ten* Commandments are paraphrased as follows: Don't have any gods before me, don't have any idols, don't take my name in vain (cursing), don't dishonor the Sabbath, don't dishonor Mom and Dad, don't steal, don't lie, don't hate (murder), don't lust (adultery and greed), and don't covet. Generation after generation in Israel could not keep the commandments. God would punish them but always preserved a remnant of his chosen people. One day, God sent Jesus to be the Savior, the long-awaited Messiah of the people of Israel, and eventually, he also became the Savior of the Gentiles (non-Jews).

If you want to go to heaven, first, you must repent and ask for forgiveness of the sins you have committed against God because these same Ten Commandments apply as strongly today as they did several thousand years ago. To repent means to make a 180-degree *turn from your sins* with the intention of never repeating them. Think about doing an about face from your sins as you *turn toward God.* Remember, first and ten. *First* repent and ask God for forgiveness for violating the *Ten,* and place your trust in Christ. Otherwise, you might find yourself out of downs; your game of life will be over; you will be lost and separated forever from the Savior of the world and our Most Holy God.

Prayer: Most gracious and loving Father, thank you for the ten rules that teach me how I should live. May I put and keep you first in my life. In Jesus's precious name, amen.

FB04:
TRANSFORMATION FROM THE OUTSIDE IN

John 3:16, 4:7–26; Romans 12:2

For God so loved the world, that He gave his only begotten Son, that whosoever believes in Him, shall not perish but have everlasting life.

John 3:16

In the fall of 1980, a new wave of UGA freshman recruits came to Athens to join an average UGA team coming off a nondescript 6–5 season. One recruit was heralded as no other Georgia recruit in history. His name was Herschel Walker. However, at a preseason practice, Coach Vince Dooley turned to an assistant and said, "I'm afraid that Herschel is just a big, stiff back." Obviously, Herschel had not shown what he could do.

He entered the first game against Tennessee in the second quarter. His first hint of stardom came when a Georgia player fumbled near the sideline. Two Tennessee defenders were poised to recover the fumble, but Herschel appeared out of nowhere and landed on the ball first. In the third quarter, Herschel exploded through two linebackers and proceeded to run directly over Bill Bates for a touchdown. Bates would play thirteen years in the NFL. UGA won 16–15, and the team knew when number 34 Walker was in the lineup, they had a chance to beat anybody.

Herschel transformed the Bulldogs into national contenders and led the team to a perfect 12–0 season and a national championship. There hasn't been one like him at Georgia before or after, but someday there will be a back that will eclipse Herschel's records. By the way, Herschel accomplished all of these feats as a child of God, a born-again Christian.

There hasn't been one like Jesus Christ. Jesus also came from the outside because he was from *outside the world*, not of this world. Jesus was not a product of this world. Jesus Christ came into the world as the Messiah, though he certainly didn't look like the Messiah that the Jews expected. The Jews expected a powerful ruler on a white horse, not a helpless baby. (Note: That version is coming later.) But Jesus provided the world with the Transformation with a capital T that it so desperately needed.

Jesus can bring you that same transformation, but first he must come from the outside into your life. Jesus first brought transformation for the woman at the well by helping her see the reasons that she was a sinner, which convinced her of her need for God's grace. She received forgiveness from Jesus and couldn't quit telling others about the living water that Jesus gave her. The only way that Jesus can come inside is by allowing his precious blood that washed on the cross to cover your sins when you repent. Repentance simply means turning from sin and wanting nothing to do with it any longer. You can't be saved by repentance, but you can't be saved without it. Once you repent and invite Christ into your life, God sends a person, the Holy Spirit, to live inside you. You will still sin because no one is perfect, but you will no longer be held in condemnation for your sin. Ask God for forgiveness and a fresh transformation daily through prayer and his holy Word to keep you in tune with his perfect plan for your life.

Prayer: Dear heavenly Father, I am so grateful that Jesus came from the outside into my heart to transform me. Now that Jesus is in my heart and the Holy Spirit lives in me, help me be transformed daily through the power of prayer and the Bible. In Jesus's name, amen.

FB05:
CLING TO THE ROCK

Psalm 62:6–7, Matthew 7:24–27

I will liken him to a wise man, who built his house upon a rock.

Matthew 7:24

The University of Georgia won the National Championship in 1980 behind the heroic performances of sensational freshman running back Herschel Walker. I still tease Becca that I married her for good luck after the 1980 season, because she went to every game with me, and UGA went 12–0. But the 1981 season would kick off at Clemson's Death Valley. There was a tremendous amount of excitement because Clemson had its best team ever, and tickets were very difficult to find. Becca and I searched outside the stadium for almost two hours and managed to find two in Section GG just before kickoff. On the way to the stadium, I asked a fan where Section GG was. He laughed and said, "Oh, that's green grass. You're on the hill that the Clemson team runs down." Becca and I managed to squeeze our way to the top of the hill with the Clemson behemoths just a few feet from us.

That's when I spied the Death Valley Rock. Frank Howard, the legendary coach of the Tigers for many years, placed a rock from Death Valley, California, in Clemson's Death Valley to create an intimidating aura for opposing teams. The monument for the rock was concrete and about four feet square. I cleverly told Becca that we could sit with our backs against the monument and watch the game. When the team ran down the hill, I patiently waited until the last player came by me. But nobody else did. The Clemson students swarmed the hill to get good seats behind the goalpost. I was bumped and lost my balance. I realized that Becca was being swept away from me and was in danger of being trampled. Reflexively, I reached and grabbed the rock with my left hand, and I wrapped my right arm around her waist. Becca was really upset, and we never did sit against the monument. In fact, we didn't even sit on the hill. We wandered around for a quarter and finally squeezed into the other end zone. The Dawgs turned it over nine times and lost the number one ranking to the eventual national champions, the Clemson Tigers. What a day to forget.

But don't forget this important fact from the book of Matthew. When life sweeps you off your feet and you're about to tumble down the hill, take one step, reach out as far as you can, and cling to God, the Rock of Ages. Psalm 62 proclaims that God alone is our rock, our salvation, and our refuge. Therefore, you should not be fearful when trouble comes. Don't wait until you're in trouble to reach for his help.

Prayer: Most gracious and merciful Father, thank you for always being there for me whenever I am in danger and whenever I need a friend. Thanks for holding onto me so I don't tumble down the hill. In Jesus's name, amen.

FB06:
WHO NEEDS THE O-LINE?
WE'VE GOT THE A-LINE!

Luke 15:10, Romans 8:28, Revelation 5:11

I heard the voices of many angels round about the throne…

Revelation 5:11

One of the most important aspects of a football team is the offensive line, or the o-line. When the o-line opens huge holes for the powerful, swift running backs, this group of unsung heroes makes it possible to move the ball down the field. The o-line performs another important duty when the members work together to perform a protective pocket around the quarterback when he drops back to pass. This pocket of protection keeps the quarterback from being tackled before he passes the ball to his swift set of receivers. Only during replays is it obvious that the o-line made it possible for the QB, the running backs, and the receivers to shine. Without an effective o-line, a team stands little chance to win.

Just as the o-line protects the quarterback from injury, God uses his legions of angels to keep us safe. Perhaps there have been times when you have faced grave danger but somehow you came through unscathed. When we get to heaven, I believe that we will understand just how many times the angels' line of defense, the a-line, came through for us. God likely used angels to protect Daniel in the lion's den and to protect David as the young lad slew Goliath. God used an angel, whom some believe was Jesus, to protect Meshach, Shadrach, and Abednego in the fiery furnace. Just like the o-line, the a-line is made up of unsung heroes who don't receive nearly as much press as the Holy Trinity. Even the misunderstood Holy Spirit gets more attention. That's the way it should be, but the a-line deserves credit also. Let's take time to remember the next time we're in a close scrape and God brings us through. Maybe, just maybe, there were five angels performing a pocket of protection.

Prayer: Dear God, help me realize that there are angels all around protecting me because you care about every detail of my life and are thinking about everything that happens around me. For that, I give you my deepest thanks. In Jesus's name, amen.

FB07:
ME AND JULIO,
DOWN BY THE SCHOOLYARD

Philippians 3:11–14

Forgetting the past, and looking forward to what lies ahead …

Philippians 3:13

The 2009 Alabama-LSU football game was another classic in that Deep South rivalry. Alabama trailed 15–10 late in the third quarter, and touchdowns had been hard to come by for the number-two-ranked team. But Bama was third and goal on the LSU 2-yard line when star receiver Julio Jones committed a critical error by illegally breaking the huddle. Julio had struggled in recent games, dropping passes left and right, according to Greg, a friend and staunch Alabama fan. Julio had not matched his pre-season All-American hype, and now this penalty. As Julio neared the Alabama bench, Coach Nick Saban ripped off his headphones and screamed at Julio as ninety-two thousand in Bryant-Denny Stadium and millions more watched the CBS telecast. Bama settled for a field goal and trailed 15–13 entering the fourth quarter. I wondered how Julio felt. Embarrassed? Probably. Humiliated? Perhaps. Unhappy? No doubt about it for letting his team down. Angry? That would have been me. Bama's perfect season and a trip to Atlanta for the SEC championship game hung in the balance because an LSU win could knock Alabama out of the race.

I was in Athens at Jillian's sorority parents' day dinner when I saw Julio commit the penalty. I was in the lobby, checking my bids on the silent auction. Not really. I was in the lobby watching the game on a big screen TV that was in the bar across the patio. I went back to our table and pulled out my BlackBerry to follow the score. A few minutes later, I clicked for an update and could hardly believe my eyes when I read, "TD 74 yard pass Julio Jones from Greg McElroy, Alabama 21 LSU 15." I am no Alabama fan, but I smiled and nodded. "Now that is a bounce back!" In fifteen minutes, Julio "went from the outhouse to the penthouse," as Vince Dooley once said when asked about the nature of the college coaching profession. Julio obviously did not allow his big failure to keep him from taking advantage of an opportunity to achieve a big success. He put the penalty behind him, remained focused, and made a play that helped his team achieve an important win.

The Apostle Paul gave a similar message to the people of Philippi when he said, "I am focusing all my energies on this one thing. Forgetting the past and looking forward to what lies ahead." Certainly Paul chose not to look back and dwell on his past failures when he had persecuted Christians. If you worry about the past, you will miss opportunities that God presents each day so that you can shine your light for all to see. If you sincerely confess your sinful mistakes and refuse to grovel in the land of self-pity and what could have been, God will forgive you, because Christ already paid the penalty for your sins and shortcomings. When you are sad, angry, depressed, humiliated, and embarrassed, remember that there is always hope for you as a believer through Jesus Christ. Let's learn from Julio's two plays. The next time you receive a setback that discourages you, talk to God about it. He alone can help you put that setback behind you so that you can look ahead to your next opportunity and his next blessing.

Prayer: Dear Father God, when I get punched in the gut unfairly by life, as I struggle to get my breath back and stay true to you, may I realize that the presence of the Holy Spirit in me is there to help me overcome the setback and others that I will face. Thank you that you live in me, to guide and protect me. In Jesus's holy name, amen.

FB08:
GUT CHECK

Matthew 26:36–44, 27:32–50

And He left them, and went away again, and prayed the third
time …

Matthew 26:43

The most successful football coaches get the maximum effort out of
their defense when they need it most: at the most crucial time of the
game. Exhausted, bone weary, injured, bloody, and bruised, the defensive unit must summon strength and courage to make the last stand.
Fourth and goal on the one-yard line, the defensive team is leading by
four, but the opponent has time for one more play. The ball is given to
the star running back, who hurdles the line only to be stopped by the
desperate lunge of a 215-pound linebacker, who drives the runner back
only six inches short of a touchdown.

In December 2009, the top two teams, number two, Alabama,
and number one, Florida, met in the Georgia Dome, just as the top
two teams, number two, Alabama, and number one, Penn State, met
in a domed stadium, the Louisiana Superdome, thirty years earlier.
Alabama fans remember how linebacker Barry Krauss, number 77,
drilled a Penn State runner just short of the goal line and won the
National Championship for Alabama in the 1979 Sugar Bowl. Krauss
hit the running back so hard that he knocked himself out. The play

has been immortalized in paintings and photographs for three decades, and the goal line play was nicknamed "gut check." I remember exactly how and where I sat in the floor when I saw the play on TV. Barry Krauss became a sideline reporter for the Alabama Football Network.

The first gut check for Jesus came in the garden of Gethsemane. Satan tried everything in his power to get Jesus to cave in so that he could score the deciding touchdown against mankind, but Jesus refused to yield to Satan. Jesus prayed to his Father in heaven on the first three downs, "Not My Will, but Thy Will be done." Jesus drank symbolically from the cup of sin that he would take to the cross that morning. Jesus struggled so mightily to block Satan that great drops of blood came from his brow. Jesus endured a blood-soaked, savage beating at the hands of the Roman soldiers and struggled mightily to drag the cross through the streets of Jerusalem. On fourth down, Jesus was nailed to the cross and hung for six excruciating hours. He could have called for a thousand legions of angels to take him off the cross and kick everybody's butt who had ridiculed, abused, and tortured him. Your sin and my sin nailed him to that cross, but love kept him there. On the cross, Jesus played a thousand fourth down gut checks each time he struggled to take his next breath to hang a little longer to demonstrate the power of his love for fallen mankind. After the skies turned black, Jesus hung for three hours, the equivalent of a football game, before he gave up the Spirit.

The next time you face a gut check and you think you can't get through it, know that Jesus already hung to make you strong. He has *been there* and *done that* just for you so that you can handle stress and strain like a saint, even discovering joy in the midst of your trials.

Prayer: Dear Jesus, I can never repay you for your gut checks that occurred because of my sin. But I thank you with all my heart and give you my life for the ultimate price you paid for me. Thank you for your amazing love and grace, and may I live in humility and gratitude for you from this moment forward. In Jesus's name, amen.

FB09:
GOD'S PERFECT TIMING

Galatians 4:4, Nehemiah 2:5, Daniel 9:25

But when the fullness of time had come, God sent his Son ...

Galatians 4:4

In a sports contest, timing means the difference between victory and defeat. Consider a pass in football when the receiver runs an out pattern by running ten yards, planting his inside foot, and cutting sharply at 90 degrees to the sideline. The quarterback must time the receiver's steps and deliver the football before the receiver comes out of his break. He leads him so that the ball arrives at the precise moment that the receiver turns to catch the ball and drags his toes to stay in bounds. The cornerback closely covers the receiver. If the throw is late or behind the receiver, it's down the sidelines for a pick six (interception for a touchdown). The timing must be perfect for the play to succeed.

God is the master of perfect timing. He sent his Son, Jesus Christ, at the perfect time. Several positive factors were already in play when Jesus arrived as a baby born to a virgin in a stable. The people of Israel were frustrated by Roman rule and eager for the Messiah that their prophets had foretold. The language of the day in numerous countries was a Greek blend, which made it easier for the first Christians to communicate the good news of the gospel that Christ rose from the dead. The Roman government had built thousands of miles of roads and aqueducts that literally paved the way for the apostles and disciples of Christ to travel from country to country. Greek philosophers left the Greek people unfulfilled. All of these factors benefited the spreading of the good news.

But the reason that God's timing is perfect is because Jesus came from heaven to earth at precisely the exact time to fulfill the prophecies of the Scripture. King Artexerxes ordered the rebuilding of the Temple walls in 445 BC. The book of Daniel predicted that the Messiah would arrive after sixty-nine "weeks." Each week actually represented a seven-year period, or 69 x 7 = 483 years. Mathematicians and astronomers studied the pattern of the new moons and discovered that Jesus rode triumphantly into Jerusalem on the back of the donkey on the very day that was predicted almost five hundred years before. Our God is a mighty God. His plan for each day of your life is replete with timing. When you get in lock step with God by surrendering your life to his guidance, he has greater blessings in store for you than you could ever imagine. He will deliver those blessings in his perfect time.

Prayer: I believe that you made the universe in six days and rested on the seventh. Help me trust that you alone know what is best for me each day, because I am your beloved child, for which I am eternally grateful. In the holy name of Jesus Christ, my Savior and Lord, amen.

FB10:
THE PRE-GAME SPEECH

1 Corinthians 2:1–5, 9:24–25; Philippians 3:14

And my speech and my preaching was not with enticing words of man's wisdom, but in demonstration of the Spirit and of power.

1 Corinthians 2:4

There have been many great pre-game speeches in the history of sports. Perhaps the most famous speech is "Win One for the Gipper." Legendary Notre Dame football coach Knute Rockne exhorted his players to win the game for their fallen teammate, George Gipp, the Gipper. On another occasion, Gale Sayers gave a very emotional speech to his Chicago Bears teammates for teammate Brian Piccolo, who would die of cancer later that season. Coach Dale, in the movie *Hoosiers,* told his basketball team that they could beat the large high school teams. He fired up his team, who came charging out of the tunnel. These talks were characterized by a person really believing passionately in their team and their cause, pleading with teammates and players to give all that they had to win the game.

The Apostle Paul pled passionately with the people of his day to win the game of life, the ultimate race and the ultimate prize. The winner receives a one-way, all-expense-paid trip to heaven and gets his or her name in the official scorebook, the Book of Life. The way to win the game of life is to surrender your heart to Christ after professing godly sorrow for your sins. God sent his Son to die for you. When you have your big game and one of God's coaches, a preacher, youth pastor, or evangelist, exhorts you to commit your life to Christ, you can come charging out of the tunnel to live for him. Are you concerned that you won't know how to play the game after you commit? Don't worry. God will take you just as you are and train you to be a Christian. As Super Bowl winning coach Tony Dungy once pointed out, God gave us his perfect Word, the Bible, to teach us how to live. He gave us prayer so that you can talk to God during the game of life anytime that you want. You can come boldly to the throne in the name of Jesus Christ to seek his guidance and listen to his advice. God gives you teammates, who are fellow believers, to help guide and transform you.

The next time you hear a pre-game speech (sermon), may it be the one that transforms you and sends you charging into the game of life for Christ.

Prayer: Father God, thank you so much for the people that you place in my life to coach me and exhort me to do greater things for your kingdom. May I have the discernment to execute on their godly instructions and wisdom. In Jesus's name, amen.

FB11:
TWO-MINUTE DRILL

1 Corinthians 9:22, 2 Corinthians 5:17, James 4:14–15

For what is your life? It is even a vapor that appears for a little time, and then vanishes away.

James 4:14

A football team that trails late in the fourth quarter employs the two-minute drill. Made famous by Baltimore Colts quarterback Johnny Unitas in the 1958 NFL Championship game, this offensive tactic is designed to move the ball quickly downfield with a series of quick passes. After each play, the offense hurries to the line of scrimmage to save precious time on the clock. One more pass is completed, and the clock ticks six, five, four, three seconds. The quarterback takes the snap, spikes the ball into the turf, and trudges wearily off the field as the field goal kicker comes in to try to save the game with a last-second miracle kick. But why did the team wind up in such a desperate predicament? Perhaps it was because of a series of fumbles, interceptions, penalties, and missed opportunities in the first fifty-eight minutes of the game. This accumulation of errors made it necessary to deploy the hurry-up offense to atone for squandered chances.

How does your walk with Christ look today? Have you lost precious time on the clock to serve him? Do you need a last-second miracle to save you? Perhaps you say, "Oh, I'm (your age). I have (seventy minus your age) years to get right with Jesus. Until then, I'll have my fun." That is a risky position to take. God gives you today. His mercies are new every morning. Jesus took the final spike two thousand years ago so that you could be free of all of the mistakes, the botched personal relationships, bad business deals, selfish decisions, and all the times you've put yourself ahead of him and your loved ones.

Here is a two-minute drill that can save your life right now, right where you're sitting, for eternity. Stop and reflect for a moment. Why is this not the perfect time to shed my old life for a new life in Christ? You don't have to be in church to come to Christ. You don't need to accomplish one more thing in your life or perform another good deed. God will take you right where you are, no matter how old or young you are. You just need to tell God in your own words how truly sorry you are that you have lived a sinful life. Then tell him that you want a new life in Christ, whom you believe died on the cross for your sins, and he will give you that fresh start.

I invite you to pray this prayer, and it's the attitude of your heart that matters most. "Lord Jesus, I realize that I can't do it my way any longer. I have sinned against you and God, and I need you to cleanse me now with the blood that you shed on the cross for me. You paid my penalty so that I don't get penalized for eternity. Please come into my new heart and give me a new life. Take control and start making me the person you want me to be. Thank you for making me a child of God and for the free gift of grace that I do not deserve but readily accept. You made my new life possible when you died on the cross and rose from the grave. In Jesus's holy and precious name, amen."

Two minutes. That's all it took to change your life for eternity. If you believe that you sincerely took off the old self and put on the new self, go tell somebody right now so that you can receive support and prayer.

Prayer: Father God, how marvelous is your grace that it costs me only two minutes to get right with you forever. But it cost Jesus his life and searing pain and agony, and I thank you for sending Jesus to die for me. Thank you, Jesus, for paying the penalty for me. In Jesus's name, amen.

FB12:
GOD'S PLAYBOOK

Psalm 12:6–7, 2 Timothy 3:16

The words of the Lord are pure words: as silver tried in a furnace of earth, purified seven times.

Psalm 12:6

One of the teenagers in Sunday school class boldly proclaimed that the Bible has many contradictions, particularly in the book of Leviticus. At the time, I didn't explain well why the Bible is indeed the perfect Word of God that was inspired by God. I did say that there are a lot of things that I don't understand, but I accept what is in the Bible by faith.

Afterward, I thought of a sports analogy. Let's suppose that the playbook of a football team contains two hundred different plays. Suppose one player decided that he didn't like play number fourteen and ripped it out of the playbook. The offensive coordinator calls for play number fourteen on the last play of the ball game even though it hadn't been used all season. Guess who didn't know where to line up. It cost the team a delay-of-game penalty, and the player was benched for the next game. Suppose a lineman chose to change the blocking scheme for a pass play. He doesn't pick up the blitzing linebacker, who blindsides his quarterback. The quarterback winds up with a concussion and is out for the season. Obviously, you cannot have players changing or deleting plays in the playbook or chaos will reign.

So why do people change the Bible to suit their needs? By ignoring certain books of the Old Testament, essentially tearing plays out of God's playbook, you will never understand how the New Testament meshes perfectly with the prophecies of the Old Testament. When you consciously apply your interpretation, you put yourself above God.

The Way of the Master Bible by evangelist Ray Comfort provides excellent guidance in helping Christians tackle many challenging and difficult interpretations of the Bible. I realize that God's ways are above my ways. To the best of my ability, I believe that God's playbook, the Bible, is inspired by God, spoken by him through more than forty authors of sixty-six books that came together seamlessly over a fifteen-hundred-year period. Either you believe the Bible is the truth, the whole truth, and nothing but the truth or it's a complete lie. Friends, there is no middle ground.

When Billy Graham was a young preacher, he had doubts about portions of the Bible. But one moonlit night, Billy got on his knees in a field and told God that he didn't understand it all but from that point forward, he would believe it all. No more changing plays or ripping plays out of the playbook for young Billy. It's no wonder at all that soon, his preaching and career as an evangelist took off.

Do you believe all the plays in God's playbook? That decision will have a major impact on God's ability to use you as a major player in his offense to advance his kingdom. God's playbook is our guide for Christian discipleship. There is a reason that the Bible has withstood the test of time. When this world ends, two things will live in the new heaven. Those two things are believers and the living Word of God. God spoke the Word into being, and the Word later became flesh in Christ (John 1:14). Since Jesus was and is perfect, then the living Word of God is perfect. The case is closed.

Prayer: Father God, thank you for your perfect Living Word. May I yearn for the knowledge that is obtained through the study of your precepts. You have given us your perfect playbook that each person can follow for wisdom, discernment, and living a life that brings glory and honor to you. In Jesus's name, amen.

FB13:
NONE GO UNDEFEATED
(SAVE ONE)

Isaiah 45:5, 22; Romans 3:23; 1 John 5:21

I am the Lord, and there is no other. There is no God besides me.

Isaiah 45:5

The 2009 college football regular season ended with a modern-day record: five unbeaten teams. The fan bases were all fired up, and when each team eventually lost again, it's a sure thing that some fans screamed, "Why did you call that pass play on third and goal?" Oklahoma won forty-seven in a row in the 1950s, but when OU finally lost 7–0 in Norman, the OU fans sat in stunned silence that their team could possibly lose a game.

No team stays undefeated. No person stays unblemished. When you make someone an idol, it is inevitable that the person will eventually let you down. No matter how hard Israel tried to keep the Ten Commandments with their 613 laws, nobody could do it, not even Saul of Tarsus.

The higher you put somebody on a pedestal and the more you live your life through a person, the greater the shock when that person falls short physically, morally, or spiritually. It's very dangerous to worship idols because you set yourself up for heartache and disappointment.

I remember vividly when I was twenty-two years old when my idol, Pete Maravich, blew out his knee at the zenith of his career. The Atlanta Hawks traded Pete to the expansion New Orleans Jazz, and the Jazz had never made the playoffs. But the Jazz rode an eight-game winning streak, and the city was abuzz with playoff fever. With a few minutes to play and the Jazz up by twenty over Buffalo, Pete entertained the Superdome crowd by whipping a between-the-legs pass down court to a teammate for a slam dunk. But the courtside patrons heard a sickening pop. Pete grabbed his right knee and writhed in pain.

I was listening to the game on a scratchy AM radio as I often did. I had pulled for Pete to have success because he was tagged a loser by some, even though he was the franchise player. In just four days, Pete would have returned to Atlanta for the NBA All-Star Game as basketball's best player at the time. Pete would show the Hawks how wrong they were to trade him, coming back to star in my city, and I would be at the game to see it all. It just was not fair. I went to the game, but I had a strange, detached feeling.

That type of reaction occurs when your goals that are totally outside your control are not realized. The reaction happens when you god up an idol and put the idol above God, breaking the first two of the Ten Commandments. I didn't know Jesus Christ when I was twenty-two. But that's where knowing Christ would have given me a huge advantage. As a believer, you remember that Jesus is number one after the disappointment and realize that no matter who or what disappointed you, your future is secure in heaven thanks to the One who took your place.

Pete never reached the same level of play after the injury and bitterly quit basketball several years later after never achieving his goal of playing for a world champion. But he found joy and peace in Jesus Christ after his playing days. Today, Pete Maravich's name is still in many record books, and it's in the only record book that matters: the

Book of Life. And so is mine. How about yours? God planned before you were born for your name to be there too.

Prayer: Father God, may I maintain perspective when I am disappointed by my team and my favorite athlete or when someone I love hurts me. May I remember the eternal game that I won when I repented and accepted Christ, and may I forgive as you forgave me for my sins through Jesus's death on the cross. In Jesus's holy name, amen.

FB14:
TIM TEBOW

Philippians 1:6

Being confident of this very thing, that He who has begun a good work in you will complete it until the day of Jesus Christ.

Tim Tebow became the first-ever college sophomore to win the famed Heisman trophy in the seventy-three years of the award. He played four years at the University of Florida and received All-American honors. Tebow currently plays quarterback for the Denver Broncos of the NFL. Upon receiving the 2007 Heisman Trophy, Tim offered these reflections on the priority in his life of football and the award.

"I'd just like to first start off by thanking my Lord and Savior, Jesus Christ, who gave me the ability to play football and gave me a great family and a support group and great coaches and everything around me," a breathless Tebow said at the ceremony, moments after the award was announced.

Football rates a mere fourth on his list of priorities behind God, family, and academics. In a profile aired on ESPN during the Heisman award ceremony, Tebow said that his priorities are, "Number one, my faith in God; number two, my family and my relationships with my family; number three, academics; and number four is football."

Prayer: Dear Father, it is so refreshing when a famous athlete has the proper perspective of priorities in his life. May Tim continue to reach many people throughout his career for the kingdom of God. In Jesus's holy name, amen.

FB15:
RUN, FORREST!

Genesis 39:7–21, Matthew 5:23–28, 1 Corinthians 6:18–20

Run from sexual sin!

1 Corinthians 6:18

One of the most memorable movies of the past few decades was *Forrest Gump*. Tom Hanks played the role of a young man from Greenbow, Alabama, who suffered from a mild form of autism. Yet everything he did turned to gold, from buying a shrimp boat in Bayou Le Batre, to saving the life of Lieutenant Dan in Vietnam, to becoming a professional table tennis player after rehabbing from being shot in the "butt-ocks."

The movie opens with Forrest as a young boy being teased mercilessly by the neighborhood boys for being slow-witted and having braces on both legs. As his young friend Jenny screams, "Run Forrest!" Forrest runs frantically to escape them. His leg braces literally disintegrate and fly from his legs as he pulls away from the boys. His next running escapade occurs when he plays football for the University of Alabama. Forrest fields a kickoff and runs toward the sideline as the coaches and players frantically direct him to run toward the goal line. He scores and runs through the end zone and out of the stadium. When his beloved Jenny leaves him after reconnecting as adults, Forrest runs to forget her. He runs across the United States and starts the jogging craze.

There is one place in the Bible that says we are to run from sin. Paul exhorted the people of Corinth who were accustomed to immoral sexual practices to "Run from sexual sin!" These people were sinning, and Paul yelled at them to run from their evil ways. Paul shouted at them like the Alabama players, coaches, fans, and the way his dear mother and his Jenny did: "Run, Forrest!" That picture is a good one to keep in your mind when your eyes linger for a second look and your mind starts to wander. Avoid that second look, turn away, and run.

Potiphar's wife tried to seduce Joseph. When she grabbed his garment and begged him to be with her, he fled. Although Joseph was wrongly accused and placed in prison, he also was shown great mercy by God and became the second most powerful man in Egypt. When you run from sexual sin, it might not seem like much, but God will reward you for that small victory. God has a special mate picked out for you, and the more you entrust your thoughts to honorable ways when temptation arises the more special that relationship will become for you. If you continuously cave into sexual temptations, you will distort your view of the opposite sex, damage your future relationship, or miss it altogether.

There was one time in the movie that Forrest should have run, but he didn't. Jenny walked into Forrest's bedroom one evening and seduced him. She later gave birth to his son. Having sex outside of marriage is a sin according to the Bible. Most Hollywood filmmakers and TV producers create storylines that would lead you to believe that there are no negative consequences from premarital sex. Making a vow to abstain from sex until marriage may seem weak in the eyes of the world, but in God's eyes it is very honorable and demonstrates obedience to him.

Keep yourself pure and honorable by running from sexual sin, and God will honor you with blessings that are much better than cheap thrills.

Prayer: Father God, never has there been a time with more temptations to commit lustful sins. Keep me strong in my daily decisions to run from sexual sin and run to you and your Word. I believe that you will honor those right decisions one day through my future relationship with the person who is just right for me. In Jesus's holy and precious name, amen.

FB16:
CHRISTMAS IN ALABAMA

2 Corinthians 4:18, Romans 8:18,
1 Thessalonians 4:13–17, Revelation 21:1–5

We look not at what can be seen, but what cannot be seen. For what can be seen is temporary, but what cannot be seen is eternal.

2 Corinthians 4:18

When I was a kid in Middle Georgia, on Christmas Day, my family would have Santa Claus and our Christmas tree, pack our suitcases, and be on the road to northwest Alabama by nine o'clock. Each Christmas Day, my mother would meet her brothers and sisters at my grandmother's house in Hamilton, Alabama, which was 387 miles of lonely, two-lane roads away. I decided back then that I would never travel with my family on Christmas Day.

One Christmas Day, we couldn't find a restaurant open to get a hamburger. Dad pulled up to a greasy spoon around two in the afternoon. He decided not to go inside because they served beer. That was admirable and made a lasting impression on me, but I was still hungry.

When I was eight, Santa brought me a full football uniform with shoulder pads and padded football pants and new cowboy boots. I wanted so badly to go out in my yard and play with my football and feel the ground as my pads collided with the grass, but there wasn't time. We had to go to Alabama. We needed to leave then or we would be late for supper. Who cares? Guess what I wore for the next 387 miles? Finally, we pulled up the gravel driveway at my grandmother's house. I leaped out of the car and begged my brother to throw me a pass after nine hours of anticipation.

Do I look forward to the celebration of the birth of Jesus with the same anticipation and excitement? Do I have that same type of longing for the Second Coming of our Savior and Lord? Look around us at the pain, suffering, and humiliation that this world brings. The book of Revelation assures us that there will be no more sorrow and no more pain forever. The Bible assures us that complete joy will be ours one day when we know Christ and he knows us. But we will not look forward daily to his coming or our departure if we allow the temporary trappings of this world to dominate our thoughts.

When is the last time you thought of eternity? If you are not a believer, eternity is the last thing that you think about because you don't want to face the truth. If you are a believer, you should look forward eagerly with anticipation to the new heaven and the new earth when Jesus comes to reign supreme, sort of like I did when I eagerly caught my first pass after waiting all day. I hope that you wait eagerly to see Jesus face to face.

Prayer: Father God, thank you for the memories of the special Christmas presents that stay fondly with me through the years. Most of all, thank you for the birth of your Son who came to save me. Help me live in a way that I eagerly wait for my face-to-face meeting with Jesus, either in heaven or in the clouds, should he come back first. In Jesus's name, amen.

FB17:
HEISMAN HYPE

Joshua 1:8, Matthew 7:7, Philippians 4:19, 2 Corinthians 4:18

But my God shall supply all your need according to his riches in glory by Christ Jesus.

Philippians 4:19

For the past seventy years, the New York City Downtown Athletic Club has awarded the Heisman trophy to the player who is selected as the top collegiate football player in America. Note that I did not say the best player, because the best player in the country is more likely to achieve success in the NFL than the typical Heisman winner. Winning the Heisman trophy has never guaranteed the same level of success in the NFL. Heisman winners Doug Flutie and Johnny Rodgers actually began their careers in the inferior Canadian Football League. Still others had mediocre careers in the NFL. Rarely does the Heisman winner turn out to be the MVP in the NFL.

The Bible teaches us that there is no guarantee of success without God and Jesus Christ at the center of our lives. Joshua 1:8 instructs us to do according to all that is written in the Bible. How will we ever know to do all that is written in it unless we *know* all that is written in it? Don't be discouraged if you know very little of the Bible in the beginning. The main point is to read or meditate on Scripture each day, and it might be for only a few minutes.

If we love God and are obedient to God by trying to do all that is written in the Bible, we will receive prosperity. It will not be prosperity as the world measures it (fame, money, awards, plaques, and trophies) but as God measures it through our willingness to share his love with our fellow man. For then we will not only find prosperity and riches, but we will know success as God measures success. Our achievement of success as believers will one day manifest itself in a special crown that awaits us in heaven.

Satan hypes stuff that we can see and touch as the key to happiness, but that hype is untrue. The college football Heisman winner is hyped as the greatest player, but he has no guarantee of success in the NFL. As a believer, you are guaranteed success as a disciple of Christ at your next level, which is the eternal level because the Holy Spirit lives within you. Once you receive Christ, you are eternal and will live forever with him.

God promises you untold riches in accordance with his plan for your life and through his mercy and grace. If you discover where God is working, he will use you to achieve victories for his kingdom. No Heisman winner will ever have anything on you.

Prayer: Dear most gracious and loving Father, help me discover the real riches that you have planned for me, not the earthly trappings that men gloat over but the internal riches of peace, joy, and love. Only through you and your Son can I ever achieve the good tidings of success and prosperity that come through a personal relationship with the Trinity. In Jesus's name, amen.

FB18:
THE POST-GAME
PRESS CONFERENCE

Psalm 7:11–13, Romans 2:1–16, 2 Peter 2:9

The Lord knows how to deliver the godly out of temptations, and to reserve the unjust to the day of judgment to be punished.

2 Peter 2:9

Imagine that you are the head coach of a major college football team with a fervent fan base. Your team just suffered its fifth consecutive loss to your bitter in-state rival. Your team committed four turnovers and performed with a lackluster effort in the second half as you got your doors blown off 48–17 at home, and your fans left in droves in the middle of the third quarter. Now it's time to face the music of the post-game press conference. As you trudge toward the press conference room, you recall that tomorrow night, you get to spend a whole hour with some of the most frustrated fans in the country on your statewide call-in show.

Who among us could stand up to the heat that comes from press conferences, call-in shows, blogs, and chat boards? How did you lose control of your team? When are you going to fire your offensive coordinator? Why did your players quit in the fourth quarter? Rumors swirl around the state that you will be fired by sundown tomorrow. What would be your reaction to all of these rumors? About 99.9 percent of us would be completely overwhelmed if we were suddenly thrust into a situation for which we are totally unprepared.

You had better believe that the coach's post-game press conference is a tough situation in those circumstances. But one day you could find yourself in a situation that is much tougher and infinitely more important and fearful. That's when you take the stand at the day of judgment. Each man and woman passes from this earth and comes before God one on one at the throne of our most holy God. Unless…

Jesus turns to the Questioner and says, "I will take all of your questions." That is the beauty of judgment day when you are a believer. Jesus will handle judgment day with God for you, and you will never have to face God. That alone is worth coming to Christ, isn't it? If you are not a believer, one who has earnestly turned from your sin and accepted Christ as your Savior, then you are in for one tough press conference. How could a person ever justify and explain to God about the times that he or she has been unfaithful and wasted time chasing the trappings and lures of the world? What a relief it is to know that Jesus will speak on our behalf at the pearly gates instead of silence before the abyss. This type of post-game press conference is inevitable. Prepare now.

Prayer: Father God, thank you for the perfect goodness of your mercy and grace that Jesus can represent me, a sinner washed in the blood of the Lamb. I pray to you now that (my friend) who will face you at judgment will come to know Jesus as Savior and Lord. In Jesus's name, amen.

FB19:
PRACTICE MAKES PERFECT

Philippians 1:6

Being confident of this very thing, that He who has begun a good work in you will complete it until the day of Jesus Christ.

When I was a kid in Middle Georgia, I was a big Green Bay Packers fan. I loved the green-and-gold uniforms with the oval G on the helmet. I knew the names and numbers of every starter and most of the substitutes. My friend from Wisconsin stared at me like I was from another planet when, as an adult, I rattled off the mid-1960s starting offensive line, "Skoronski 76, Thurston 63, Ringo 50, Kramer 64, and Gregg 75."

The Packers won five NFL championships in the sixties, including the first two Super Bowls, under legendary coach Vince Lombardi. Coach Lombardi was a disciplinarian and drilled into his players the need to execute plays perfectly. One play the Packers perfected was the Green Bay power sweep. The Packers would pull the right guard on running plays around left end and vice versa. This maneuver outnumbered the defenders and opened huge holes for halfback Paul Hornung and fullback Jim Taylor. No matter how the defense prepared, the Packers seemed to get the first down and touchdown they needed when they ran this play.

Training camp would open in July under miserably hot conditions. Even though the veterans knew this play like the backs of their hands, Lombardi would have them run it again and again and again. Some players probably ran the play thousands of times over the course of their careers. Lombardi didn't just run it in July and never practice it again because he knew that in December, the timing would be off and the play would break down at the most crucial time. He would no longer have his go-to play, his bread-and-butter play, without that repetitious practice.

Your life as a Christian resembles the Green Bay power sweep. You become a Christian when you get it for the first time and become converted. But the schemes that Satan throws against you each day are powerful and designed to knock you off track. That's why the discipline of daily prayer and reading the Bible and study becomes important. Sure, you know the story of the gospel by heart, and the birth of Jesus and his death and resurrection, but your timing is thrown off little by little if you don't practice daily. One day when you need it most, you find that you've lost your power because you allowed the world to rule you instead of God's plan. God even gives you an extra blocker, the Holy Spirit, to overcome Satan and rip huge holes in his defense. Your dedication and renewal each day allows you to open holes for others to become believers through your words, deeds, and actions in the name of Christ. Satan knows it's coming, but he can't stop it. Satan's strength is always weaker than God's strength. You have the supernatural strength of God when you practice daily blocking and tackling through prayer and Bible study.

Prayer: Thank you, Father God, for the power sweep o-line of God, Jesus, the Holy Spirit, prayer, and Bible study that enables me to avoid the obstacles that Satan presents. I praise you for sending me Jesus to save me from myself. In Jesus's name, amen.

FB20:
CAMPFIRE, BONFIRE,
OR FOREST FIRE?

1 Corinthians 3:9–15, Revelation 1:8–13, Colossians 3:17

> But if the house he has built burns up, he will suffer a great loss. He himself will be saved, but like a man escaping through a wall of flames.
>
> 1 Corinthians 3:15

One of the great traditions in high school and college sports is homecoming week. A big event at many homecoming celebrations on the eve of the big game is the bonfire. On Thursday and Friday fall nights on campuses across America, students, faculty, and friends thrill at the sight of a blazing bonfire as faces are warmed and friendship bonds are strengthened. Fans eagerly anticipate the exciting game the following day.

Perhaps the greatest bonfire tradition was at Texas A&M University in College Station, Texas. A team of cadets would be assigned each year to construct the bonfire, and the competition to build the tallest bonfire ever was intense. One year, the stack of wood reached over 100 feet into the sky. Unfortunately, a tragic accident occurred that resulted in the loss of precious lives, and the bonfire celebration was postponed. A wonderful tradition had unfortunately become a shocking, horrendous tragedy.

The book of Revelation promises that Jesus will look upon the words, deeds, and actions that you and I accumulate over a lifetime. Jesus will look upon our events that are stacked like cordwood. Those deeds that were performed in the name of Jesus will be purified like silver refined seven times and burnished gold and will last for eternity. Those actions that were performed for selfish reasons and personal glory will be incinerated. Poof!

Think about the life that you've lived thus far and how you spend your spare time. Maybe there is a reason you don't have spare time. Are you working for God or mostly working for yourself? If you've consistently worked for God to achieve victories for his kingdom, your fire will more closely resemble a campfire. The more selfish acts the greater the fire. Would your accomplishments turn into burnished gold or a huge bonfire or a raging forest fire? Determine from this day forward that your private time will include plenty of acts to advance God's kingdom and that you include God in your work or school. If your words and deeds include God, then they won't go up in smoke.

Prayer: Father God, thank you for the knowledge in your Word that my selfish deeds will one day go up in smoke. May I use this knowledge when I'm sitting around and have a choice to do something for me or do something for God. In Jesus's name, amen.

FB21:
ALL-ACCESS PASS

Matthew 27:51, Hebrews 4:16

And behold, the veil of the temple was torn in two from the
top to the bottom ...

Matthew 27:51

If you've ever been to a large sporting event, you'll notice that there
is a pecking order. There is a big difference between the nosebleed
and courtside seats. There is nothing like an all-access pass that allows
you to go anywhere in the arena or stadium. An all-access pass at the
Masters golf tournament is equivalent to getting into the press room,
the clubhouse, and out on the veranda near the putting green. It's cool
to even be at Augusta, but eventually, you find yourself staring at the
people on the clubhouse grounds at the tables under the giant oak tree.
You wonder what it would be like to be on the other side of the ropes.

At the 2010 BCS Championship game, an all-access pass got you
onto the field before and after the game. My daughter Allison's boy-
friend, Kevin, got a sideline pass to the Alabama-Texas game, and she
wished that she could have been there with him. At the NBA Finals,
you could stand in the tunnel next to Kobe or Lebron just before they
jog onto the floor. Anybody who has been to the Final Four would
love to be courtside to see the interaction between players, coaches,
and officials in the high-pressure game situation. An all-access pass at a

concert would get you onto the back of the stage as performers excite the crowd with well-known songs.

In the Old Testament days, the only person with an all-access pass was the chief priest. But the chief priest could only go behind the veil in the holy of holies once a year, sort of like Super Bowl Sunday comes once a year. On that day, the chief priest cleansed himself before entering the holy of holies and presenting the sacrifices before God. That was the one day a year that someone interacted with God.

But Jesus changed all of that. After God could no longer look upon the sins that his Son carried to the cross, the temple walls collapsed and that curtain was torn in two forever. The tearing of the curtain indicated that all people now had twenty-four-seven access to God through Jesus Christ, who sits as our intercessor when we talk with God. Jesus is the all-access pass that everyone needs to come boldly to God's throne.

Prayer: God, how awesome it is that I can come to you at any time, night or day, when I need to talk. Help me remember that there are many times that you want to come talk with me. In Jesus's name, amen.

FB22:
KNOCKING ON THE DOOR

Revelation 3:20, 2 Corinthians 5:17, Titus 3:5

Behold, I stand at the door and knock...

Revelation 3:20

The University of Georgia football team had a legendary announcer named Larry Munson for over forty years. Larry was best known for his dramatic, emotional calls of famous plays in Georgia history. When UGA drove down the field and got inside the opponents' 20-yard line, Munson would shout, "Georgia's knocking on the door! They're on the Tennessee sixteen!" That line reminds me of Revelation 3:20: "Behold, I stand at the door and knock. If anyone hears my voice and opens the door, I will come into him and dine with him and him with me."

Do you realize that until you become a believer, Jesus waits patiently at the door of your heart every day, knocking politely, waiting for you to invite him in? The next time you see your front door, imagine that Jesus is sitting on the doorstep, waiting to be invited into your home. However, there is no doorknob to the door of your heart on the outside. There is only a doorknob on the inside of your heart, and only you can turn it to open the door of your heart for Christ. Jesus will never force his way into your heart. If Jesus did, it wouldn't be your decision, would it? And God has given each person free will to decide how to live his or her life. Only when you say in your heart, *I am sick and tired of this sinful, hypocritical life that I'm living, and I want to shed the old me for a new me!* will Jesus come through the door and into your life for eternity. You can repent, open the door, and make him your Savior today. Come, Lord Jesus.

Prayer: Lord Jesus, thank you for waiting patiently for me each day. Father God, thank you for the second, third, fourth, and hundredth chances that you have given me. You are so loving, kind, and merciful. In Jesus's name, amen.

FB23:
WILL YOU ACKNOWLEDGE THE CLAMOR OF THE COWBELLS?

Jeremiah 1:5–6, Ezekiel 36:26, Matthew 3:1, Matthew 4:17

Before you came forth out of the womb, I sanctified you, and
I ordained you a prophet of the nations.

Jeremiah 1:5

Becca and I traveled to Tupelo, Mississippi, to spend the night with our
friends, Frank and Ginger. The next morning, we all headed to Starkville
for the Georgia-Mississippi State game. Herschel Walker was a junior,
and when Herschel played, Becca and I didn't miss a game, home or
away. We were confident that UGA would win, but Starkville presented
a unique challenge called cowbells. Thousands of Mississippi State fans
owned cowbells that were painted maroon and white and adorned with
fraternity logos and other decorations. Together, these cowbells made a
horrendous clatter. Before the game, I heard the fans rattle the cowbells.
I turned to my friend, Frank, and said, "Frank, I thought the SEC out-
lawed the use of cowbells inside the stadium. Look at those people. How
did they get those cowbells in the stadium?" Frank looked at me with
a straight face and said with all sincerity, "Cowbells? I don't hear any
cowbells." He turned to his friend Bruce and asked, "Bruce, do you hear
any cowbells?" Bruce shook his head. "Frank, I don't hear any cowbells

either." Obviously, they were both pulling my leg. UGA won the game despite the clamor of cowbells throughout the game.

Frank's remark about not hearing any cowbells is how some people react to hearing the gospel. Frank didn't acknowledge the cowbells even though he heard them because he enjoyed the advantage the noise gave Mississippi State. I sat in church for years and heard the gospel preached. I heard the preacher, but I didn't hear the gospel because I never internalized the message due to a hardened heart that kept me from hearing the message clearly. Our Methodist ministers preached a comfortable gospel that rarely mentioned sin and certainly never mentioned hell. If I wasn't hearing sin on Sunday, and I certainly wasn't reading about sin during the week, being Bible ignorant, I continued to dwell in the bliss of my ignorance.

God has sent noisemakers to clang the cowbells for thousands of years in the form of prophets, preachers, and evangelists. From John the Baptist to Isaiah to Jeremiah to Ezekiel to Daniel to Hosea, the prophets rang the cowbells, warning of the judgment to come, but so often, the message fell on the deaf ears of the Israeli people. Sadly, many people today will hear the gospel but choose not to follow Jesus because of comfortable living and hardened hearts. Praise God that I finally heard when my favorite athlete explained how he heard the good news of Jesus Christ.

If you don't know Christ, the likelihood that you will respond to the gospel decreases as you get older. You get a little deafer because your hardened heart makes the gospel bounce away. You achieve an impressive track record of worldly success but give God none of the credit. You're afraid that your good life will change if you give into living like the preacher. But your good life will eventually lead to ruin and destruction. Isn't it time that you acknowledged the clatter of the gospel cowbells and turned to Christ?

Prayer: Father God, thank you for sending the prophets of yesteryear and today to share the good news of the gospel. I pray for a new enlightenment among my friends who need Christ but refuse to hear the clang of the warning. I thank you daily for the mercy and grace you showed me and show me still. In Jesus's name, amen.

FB24:
ARE YOU DEPENDING ON A
LAST-SECOND MIRACLE?

John 6:44, Matthew 6:30, Acts 5:1–5

The Father will draw you to the Son …

John 6:44 (paraphrased)

Each fall weekend, several college or pro games are decided by a last-second field goal attempt. Either the field goal is good and the offense wins or the field goal is missed and the defense wins. The field goal kicker, the specialist of all football players, warms up his leg on the sideline and is suddenly thrust front and center under a white-hot spotlight as the opposing fans scream for the kicker to miss a kick that is usually between thirty and fifty yards. The kicker must send the ball between two posts that look no wider than a car from that distance. The game and possibly a title hang in the balance. The snapper must deliver the ball crisply to the holder. Every lineman must block well and not jump offside. The holder must catch the ball, place it on the spot, and twirl the ball to place the laces away from the kicker. The kicker must plant his foot securely and deliver a perfectly timed kick. The ball must be kicked high, far, and accurately. If the opponent doesn't block it, then the kicker's team might just win the game. Pretty simple? Hardly.

Naturally, any number of plays better executed during the game could have prevented this last-gasp effort. Will your opportunity to know Christ and receive God's free gift of grace that you can't earn hang in the balance like the team that depends on a last-second miracle kick to bail them out? *Don't depend on it.* Our God is unquestionably a merciful God, but there are stories in the Bible where God's patience ran out and he killed people. God killed Ananias and his wife for keeping part of the funds for the church. Only Noah and seven others were spared for the flood. Are you determined to keep on sinning because there is pleasure in sin and expect a bailout after you have had your fun? After missing sign after sign to turn away from sin, are you going to wait for a deathbed miracle to save you? Your plan might be thwarted by your hardened heart. You might have a heart attack and die or you might fall into a coma and never have a chance to make the eternal game-changing decision. Your foot might slip, and you could wind up in a fatal car accident. God only gives us today, and the Bible makes it clear that you are a vapor, here today and gone tomorrow.

The odds grow longer with each passing decade that you will make that game-winning kick and come to know Christ. The winning kick gets more difficult, and the conditions seem to worsen, further stacking the odds against you. As my brother in Christ, former pro wrestler Lex Luger, said to me, "We're single-digit guys." Lex meant that the odds of coming to know Christ after you are forty, as Lex and I did, are less than one in ten. I urge you to make the eternal, life-saving play the next time the Holy Spirit and God draw you to the Son. Then you can *know* you are victorious. As the final gun sounds to end your game on this earth, you can take the last snap, gracefully take a knee, raise your arms to the sky, and celebrate your victory in Jesus.

Prayer: Thank you for wooing me to your Son. Thank you for never giving up on my friends, my family members, and especially me. In Jesus's name, amen.

FB25:
EYE IN THE SKY

Isaiah 55:8–9

For as the heavens are higher than the earth, so are my ways higher than your ways, and my thoughts are than your thoughts.

Isaiah 55:8

On many football teams, the defensive and offensive coordinators sit in the press box high above the playing field. The better their view the better their understanding is of the opponent's offensive and defensive schemes. The better their understanding of the schemes the more likely that the coordinators will call the right plays. When you're at field level, the view is obscured because players are blocking your view of the game. It's difficult to see exactly where each player is positioned. If even one player's position is misunderstood, that mistake can result in a game-changing play and an easy touchdown for the opponent. Shouting and mass confusion on the sidelines distorts the coach's judgment. Sitting in the upper reaches of the press box provides an increased level of calm that results in better decision making.

NFL teams take Polaroid snapshots from high above the field of each play and fax them to the sideline. The faxed photos are placed in a three-ring binder. When the quarterback comes off the field, he can see each defensive formation from the previous drive. Those photos allow the quarterback to execute more effectively on the following drive.

God has the big picture. God has the eye in the sky and can see many things that you cannot see. You see the tip of the iceberg above the water, but God also sees the iceberg under the water. Would it not make complete sense to align with God, in effect, turn your life over to him since he knows what's coming and he knows what's best for your life? God loves you infinitely, and he already perfectly planned each day of the rest of your life. You won't be limited to your narrow, biased, myopic view of your circumstances in the world. Your personal power through Christ is unleashed when you are aligned with God's plan.

Prayer: Father God, help me surrender my life to you so that I can unleash the mighty power that you can use through me. Help me trust you and remember that my thumbnail view of a situation can't hold a candle to your infinite knowledge. In Jesus's name, amen.

FB26:
TONY DUNGY

Philippians 4:13

I can do all things through Christ who strengthens me.

After his Indianapolis Colts convincingly won Super Bowl XLI in 2007, Tony Dungy became the most respected coach in the NFL. Dungy soon retired from coaching. He became an NBC football analyst, but he also chose to spend more time making a difference for Jesus Christ. Dungy became the spokesman for All-Pro Dad, a nationwide program introduced by Family First with his help that teaches men how to become better fathers by living out Christian principles.

Notably he mentored Philadelphia Eagles quarterback Michael Vick weekly when Michael was being held in a maximum security prison in Leavenworth, Kansas. Many people believe that he helped Vick discover his new life in Christ. With Dungy by his side, Vick testified of his newly discovered faith at a Super Bowl prayer breakfast in February 2010.

Coach Dungy once explained that "the Bible is life's playbook. It provides answers to the biggest questions life has. With the Colts, we have a playbook that details exactly what we want to do. If a player is uncertain, he only has to read the playbook. The Bible is like that. When we're not sure how to act, how to deal with a certain situation, we go to the Bible to get God's plan for how it should be done. Through his Son, Jesus Christ, God has revealed how we are to live."

Prayer: Father God, thank you for the difference that a Christian brother such as Tony Dungy can make in the lives of other men. May I learn from his example of serving others, faith sharing, and discipleship. In Jesus's name, Amen.

FB27:
MARK RICHT

Jeremiah 29:11

I know the plans that I have for you, says the Lord. Plans for welfare and not for harm, to give you a future with hope.

Mark Richt has been the head football coach at the University of Georgia since 2001. He has led the Dawgs to two SEC championships and several Top 5 rankings. Coach Richt is known for his calm under pressure, his servant heart, and his willingness to share his faith with audiences across the Southeast. In March 2009, Coach Richt and Tony Dungy announced the expansion of All-Pro Dad into college football at a press conference in Athens, Georgia. Here is Coach Richt's account of how he came to a saving relationship with Jesus Christ when he was a young coach at Florida State University.

"I was into my second season (coaching) at FSU and thought that I was doing fairly well, until one fateful day in September …One of our players was shot and killed while attending a party …Coach Bowden called a team meeting …[and] pointed to the empty chair that was assigned to the fallen player, and talked about death and his faith. He asked every one of us in the room to look at the chair and then he asked, 'If that was you, do you know where you would spend eternity?'"

"I was a broken young coach, so the next day, I went to see him. He took me through the gospel and explained what it meant to be a Christian …It was time. My life had not turned out like I planned.

I understood how self-centered and prideful I was. I saw my sin revealed and the reality of God's love for me…Coach Bowden led me in a prayer that day, and I received God's mercy, forgiveness, and peace through what Christ had done for me. I understood that…I would (never) be good enough to earn God's love. It is a free gift. I left Coach Bowden's office a new man."

Prayer: Father God, thank you so much for the godly example set by Coach Richt, a man in the national spotlight who has consistently demonstrated that Jesus Christ is first in his life. May I emulate Christlike faith and grow in my love for you. In the holy and precious name of Jesus, amen.

FB28:
SHAUN ALEXANDER

Psalm 37:4

Delight yourself also in the Lord, and He shall give you the desires of your heart.

Shaun Alexander was an All-American running back at the University of Alabama during the 1996–1999 seasons. After setting numerous rushing records for the Crimson Tide, he became an All-Pro with the Seattle Seahawks and led the NFL in rushing one season. Shaun wore number 37 during his football career, and one of his favorite verses comes from Psalm 37.

Shaun was certainly blessed with as much wealth and fame as life has to offer. Yet he remarked that possessions aren't the most important things in his life.

"A rich man thinks of himself as being rich," Shaun says. "I just think of myself as being blessed. If I'm just blessed, then I'll go out and bless other people…Most kids don't know that they're supposed to be something awesome in this world, or they don't believe they can be. I play to help them understand that they are special."

Shaun has never been the one to do something just because everyone else is. "I'm always the oddball compared to everyone else," he says. "That's because I don't live by their rules. I go by God's rules."

Prayer: Father God, may I learn from Shaun's example that the true riches in life come from living by your rules and being a blessing to others. Help me remember that when I am a blessing to others, I receive a blessing in return. In Jesus's name, amen.

FB29:
HERSCHEL WALKER

Proverbs 3:5–6

Trust in the Lord with all of your heart, and lean not on your own understanding; In all your ways acknowledge Him, and He shall direct your paths.

At the University of Georgia, Herschel Walker set an NCAA freshman rushing record and helped his team capture the 1980 national collegiate football title. He earned consensus All-American honors three consecutive years and capped a sensational college career by earning the 1982 Heisman trophy in his junior year. Walker was one of the top running backs in the pros, gaining more all-purpose yards than anyone in professional football history, counting his NFL and USFL seasons.

"My message is always about how Christ is in everything," Walker said. "I talk about how on a dollar bill we have 'In God We Trust,' yet we don't put our trust in him. I talk about how we've taken religion out of everything. Let's put it back. And I talk about believing in Christ and putting faith in him and seeing where that takes you."

Prayer: Most holy and gracious God, may I put my trust in you today and take a stand for Christ, whether I am at home or with my friends. Help me learn from Herschel that trusting in Christ will lead me where I need to go. In Jesus's name, amen.

FB30:
A FINAL DADGUM TRIBUTE TO BOBBY BOWDEN

John 15:5

He that abides in me, and I in him, will bear much fruit. Apart from me you can do nothing.

Coach Bobby Bowden went out in style at the 2010 Gator Bowl as his Florida State Seminoles upset West Virginia to give Coach Bowden his thirty-fourth consecutive winning season at Florida State. About 350 of his former players were in Jacksonville to see his final game. His numbers defy description with 389 career wins, two national championships (could have been five except for field goal attempts that went wide right), twelve conference championships, and, his most incredible stat to me, fourteen consecutive top-five finishes in the polls.

Unquestionably, Florida State coach Bobby Bowden is one of the most successful college football coaches in history. But few people in the sports world have advanced the cause of Jesus Christ as this man has. For over fifty years, Bowden has accepted invitations to speak whenever and wherever he can, particularly to church groups and particularly when he is on the road with the team.

When Bobby was twenty-three, he really got the picture and re-dedicated his life to the Lord. He recalled, "As I came up, I thought that being good was being a Christian. I knew you had to join the church. I joined the church. I knew you had to be baptized. I was baptized. I thought that, plus being good, makes you a Christian.

"I finally realized that you are saved by grace. It's nothing that you did and nothing that you earned. Once I understood that, it made life simpler to me. Because, with understanding grace, it makes you want to do better. Nobody's perfect. I make mistakes every day."

The ESPN ticker often streams negative publicity about coaches. However, during Bowden's final game as head coach, we were able to enjoy three hours of fond memories and bask in the glow of what is right in college sports. The Florida State fans appreciate the wins, but they must surely appreciate even more the legacy of the man who led them to those victories. Bobby's lasting legacy is the fruit that he has borne for the kingdom of God through his grace, his faithful witness, and his perseverance.

Prayer: Most gracious Lord, it is so awesome to see that a man of Bobby Bowden's fame seeks to deflect the glory to you. May his ministry of teaching men about Jesus Christ continue to bear fruit. In Jesus's name, amen.

FB31:
BORN TO DIE

Isaiah 7:14, 9:6; Micah 5:2; Luke 2:10–16

Today a Savior, who is Messiah the Lord, was born for you in the city of David.

Luke 2:11

The 2009 Georgia high school football season ended with five schools crowned champions of their respective classifications. Notably, Buford High School won its fifth championship of the decade. Once, *Sports Illustrated* published a feature article about the winningest teams in America and anointed Valdosta, Georgia, as its Winnersville, USA. A South Georgia town on I-75 near the Florida line, Valdosta became famous under the tutelage of legendary coach Wright Bazemore, who won fourteen state titles, more than any coach in Georgia high school history.

As is the case in thousands of small towns from Georgia to Texas to California, high school football is approached with religious fervor in Valdosta. The town set the tone a generation ago when nurses at the local hospital began placing tiny gold-and-black footballs in the bassinets of its newborn males. The expectation was clear that these boys were to grow up to become Valdosta Wildcats and help bring more championships to the town. Proud daddies would train the boys at an early age to catch and run with the stuffed footballs until the lads graduated to pee wee football for formal training in blocking and tackling. If a boy didn't make the high school team, he could still play in the band or become a team manager. All should be devoted to the cause of the Wildcats. However, the demographics shifted about twenty years ago, and now Lowndes County High School has emerged as the more dominant power in the county. Perhaps parents choose between gold-and-black footballs and maroon-and-gray footballs now at the hospital.

I experienced a Christmas concert presented by the gifted Christian pianist and composer Stanton Lanier (stantonlanier.com), the founder of a nonprofit organization called Music to Light the World. Stanton uses videos to great effect as he presents his scripturally inspired compositions and provides inspirational CDs to cancer wards across the country. In his closing video, a golden silhouette line emerged from the manger and wound across the dark landscape to a cross on a hillside. Just as baby boys in Valdosta received a toy revealing an expectation to play football in their futures, the baby Jesus had a different reminder placed in the manger. God figuratively placed a cross inside the manger because from his earliest recollection as a child, Jesus understood that there was a cross in his future. Jesus knew he would fulfill the prophecies at the age of thirty-three by dying on the cross because you and I are sinners. Jesus knew that he was born to die, and he lived to demonstrate God's great mercy and grace daily. Yes, Jesus was born to die but also to be raised from the grave on the third day.

Jesus beat death forever. Today, you can beat death by turning away from your sins and receiving Christ into your life. Jesus was born to die for your sins so that you can have eternal life in heaven, eternal life that begins the moment you prepare him a permanent place in your heart. This fundamental truth is the hope that all people can have, no matter what their circumstances might be. If you are a believer, share your hope with someone who desperately needs it.

Prayer: Father God, thank you for your immeasurable love that you would send your beloved Son, Jesus Christ, to be born as a baby. He came to walk among us, love us, and experience our hurts and disappointments and took our sins to the cross of Calvary so that we could be born again. May I share my hope in Christ with others. In Jesus's holy name, amen.

FB32:
TOMMY BOWDEN

Isaiah 45:22

Let all the world look to me for salvation; for I am God, there is no other.

Tommy Bowden is the son of Bobby Bowden and was also a winning head football coach on the collegiate level at Tulane University and Clemson University. The Bowden family has long exemplified a deep-seated faith that has endured through success on the field, through adversity, and through the tragic loss of a grandson. Tommy wrote the following poem, which speaks of gratitude and Christian principles that we can use to guide us through each day.

Excerpt from *A Simple Call*
Tommy Bowden
1973

Guide and strengthen us through each day,
to act and talk in a Christ-like way.

Though we are not worthy of his awesome power,
we need it to survive each and every hour.

Boy, it is great to have a God to love,
Who's always there, just right above.

A God so great, He gave his only Son,
Yes, for me, you, and everyone.

Prayer: Most gracious and loving God, thank you for your immeasurable, incomparable, unfathomable, infinite love, which you demonstrated so incredibly through the death and resurrection of Jesus. Thank you, Father, for your peace which passes understanding that is available to each person who knows Jesus as Savior and Lord. In the precious name of our Savior, the One who took our place, amen.

BASEBALL

BB01:
THERE IS POWER IN WEAKNESS

2 Corinthians 12:6–9

The Lord said to Paul, "My grace is sufficient for you, for power is made perfect in weakness."

2 Corinthians 12:9

When I was nine, a boy named Mickey limped into the gym where Dad was practicing basketball one evening with the high school boys. His name was William Michael, but he was called Mickey after the Mick, Mickey Mantle. Mickey had a squeaky brace on his lower left leg. I found out he was born with no left calf muscle and a foot that was smaller than his other foot.

The next year, he and I were at the same elementary school, and we became instant friends because we were both sports nuts. In high school, I was the point guard, and Mickey was the shooting guard. I saw him score eighty-two points in two games in one weekend. Amazing! Mickey might have been the most intense competitor I ever faced, and his determination and athletic skills helped him earn a Division 1 baseball scholarship from the University of Georgia. God blessed him with a strong right arm and foot speed despite his left leg. When you played against Mickey, he would never admit that you had an advantage. He just played harder than you to overcome it. He never let the "thorn in his flesh" stop him from becoming a tremendous athlete who competed on the highest collegiate level.

I have always thought of Mickey as a person who showed tremendous perseverance to achieve these athletic goals. One day, Mickey's mother called for him to leave because they were late for a doctor's visit to see about his foot. When she went into his bedroom, Mickey said, "Mama, I was praying that God would heal my foot."

By the way, Mickey became a strong Christian who works hard for the youth and men in his church in Athens, Georgia. It's awesome to know that he and I will again share the playing field as brothers in Christ in heaven one fine day.

Paul didn't let his "thorn in his flesh" stop him either. God empowered Paul with the Holy Spirit to enable him to overcome shipwrecks, beatings, the thirty-nine lashes five times, and countless other hardships to spread the gospel like none before him or since.

If you have a handicap, remember that God doesn't give everybody every gift. Play to your strengths as Mickey did to overcome any "thorns in the flesh," and with God's help, you can realize your special gifts.

Prayer: Father God, all of us have a "thorn in the flesh" of some type. But help me use the strengths that you gave me to overcome it, and trust in you to help me do my best. In Jesus's holy and precious name, amen.

BB02:
RUN THE RACE TO WIN

1 Corinthians 9:24–27, Philippians 3:13–14, 1 Timothy 4:12

I strain to reach the end of the race, and receive the prize...

Philippians 3:14

I remember the play as if it happened last week. When I was twelve, my All-Star team played in the district playoffs. In the first game of a best-of-three series, with a runner on first base and two out, I hit a hard ground ball up the middle. I saw the shortstop go behind second base to make the play. I thought he would just step on the bag for the force play. But his momentum carried him past the bag, so he threw to first. I slowed down, thinking the third out had been made. As I jogged toward the first base bag, the ball slammed into the first baseman's glove. Imagine my horror being two feet from the bag when I could have been safe by a mile. My team lost that game, but fortunately, we won the next two and advanced to the state tournament.

That play taught me an important lesson. Always run through the base. Run through the tape if you are a sprinter or lunge for the wall if you are a swimmer. Michael Phelps won his most dramatic race at the Beijing Olympics by going harder into the wall than his opponent. Usain Bolt ran through the tape to set the world record.

The Apostle Paul was really into races. Though he was not a runner, perhaps due to that "thorn in his flesh," he grew up in Greece, where the early Olympics were held. Paul made numerous references to races for teaching purposes because the people understood races. In Philippians, he urged the early Christians to "strain to reach the end of the race, and receive the prize." One race that you run daily is to strive to be obedient and loving throughout each day, from beginning to end. The prize that you receive is peace of mind and the joy and satisfaction of a day well-lived for Christ. That type of race doesn't sound exciting, but when you face trials, you will be closer to God. You will know that he is there to help you run races, even marathons, which seem impossible.

Never let anyone tell you that you are too young to run the race for Christ. Paul made it very clear in 1 Timothy 4:12 that young Christians can influence their friends, classmates, and family members for Christ. Remember, in the Old Testament, Josiah became king at the ripe old age of eight.

Prayer: Father God, give me a desire to run a steady race each day for you, from beginning to end, and give you the glory. In Jesus's name, amen.

BB03:
MAKING THE ONE BOX SCORE
THAT COUNTS

Revelation 20:15, 21:27

But they which are written in the Lamb's Book of Life ...

Revelation 20:15

When I played Little League, one of the thrills of playing well in a game was to see my name in the local newspaper the following day. At five o'clock sharp, I would hurry on my bike to the post office to pick up the Dublin Courier-Herald. I knew that when I had four hits or hit a grand slam or struck out eighteen and pitched a no-hitter, my name would be in the paper for all of Laurens County to see. As you might imagine, I felt pretty darn good about my personal success. My focus was primarily on *me* and my personal accomplishments, and often I gloried in my success.

Even though I was baptized at age eleven, I did not have a personal relationship with Jesus Christ. Baptism alone doesn't make a person a Christian, just as wearing a Braves jersey doesn't make you a major league ballplayer. At the time, I didn't realize that no matter how many trophies I won or how many times I got my name in the box score, all that would really matter was if I got my name in the box score in heaven, the box score called the Book of Life, where all the names are recorded of the believers who received Christ as their Savior and Lord.

As an adolescent and adult, I continued to live for myself, getting two college degrees and a very good job. I had success as a college golfer and college basketball referee, and I even started a popular basketball program at Mt. Zion UMC. God blessed me with my soul mate, Becca, and two wonderful daughters, Allison and Jillian. But as a supposedly mature adult, I continued to seek the accolades of men, until I realized at forty-eight that it wasn't about me. It was about Jesus and how he died on the cross for me. God forgave me for all the times that I had lied, cheated, stolen, put myself above him, and blasphemed his name on the golf course and basketball court. When I was drawn to Christ that night by the Holy Spirit, I exchanged my sinful self for a new person in Christ. Now my name is in the only record book that matters: the Book of Life.

Prayer: Dear heavenly Father, thank you for writing my name in the only book that matters, the Book of Life, and for all of the saints who came before me. In the name of Jesus, amen.

BB04:
THE "NOT SO PERFECT" PERFECT GAME

Philippians 1:6; Matthew 5:48; Romans 12:2;
Psalm 19:12, 51:10

He who has begun a good work in you will complete it until the day of Jesus Christ.

Philippians 1:6

In 2009, Chicago White Sox hurler Mark Buehrle pitched a perfect game that was highlighted by a miracle catch by a reserve outfielder who made a leaping catch at the wall in the ninth inning, bobbling the ball and spearing it just above the surface of the warning track. It occurred to me that Buehrle's game wasn't really perfect after all. Perfection would be eighty-one consecutive strikes with no fair balls hit. Buehrle threw forty pitches out of the strike zone, and twenty-one of twenty-seven batters put the ball in fair territory, including the four-hundred-foot blast that almost left the park.

Buehrle's perfect game reminded me of my no-hitter and almost perfect game in Little League. Here was my pitching line that night against the Cubs.

Name	IP	H	R	ER	BB	K	LOB
Farr	6	0	0	0	0	18	1

Everything was on for me that night. I had pinpoint control of my fast ball, and my concentration was fine tuned. It appears that I struck out every hitter, but I didn't. I struck out the first sixteen Cubs and had a 1–2 count on the eighth hitter at the bottom of the lineup. I thought, *I'm gonna do it. Four more strikes, and I'll have a* perfect, *perfect game!* I delivered the 1–2 fast ball, and to my horror, the batter swung late and drilled a ground ball right at my first baseman, who let it go under his glove and right through the wicket. I looked anxiously at Steve Jessup, the scorer for the game, in the press box. After some deliberation, Steve ruled an error on the play. My buddy for life. I struck out the final two batters of the game to preserve my no-hitter.

Perhaps during a day you think, *Wow, I've really been good today. I don't believe that I've sinned even once in the past four hours. I'm pitching a perfect game!* Well, your perfect day is probably not so perfect because God looks at your thoughts, your motives, and your actions. God holds you responsible for lustful thoughts, selfish motives, impure actions, and being self-absorbed with me, me, me. Realize that the thought process is why it is so important to transform your mind continuously each day because Satan wants to push impure thoughts into your mind nonstop.

Whenever you think you're pitching a perfect game, that moment is a perfect time to go to God and ask for forgiveness for your self-righteousness. While you are there, ask God to search for sins that lurk in your heart that you don't even know are there and let him create a clean heart in you. And on the final day, if you know Jesus, God will make you perfect, as Jesus is perfect, when he completes what he started in you (Philippians 1:6).

Prayer: Dear Lord God Almighty, maker of the universe, may I seek perfection through loving you and being obedient to you. When I fall short, may I come readily to you for a fresh cleansing with the blood of the Lamb. In Jesus's holy and precious name, amen.

BB05:
DON'T COUNT ON THE CURVE

Exodus 20:1–17, John 14:6, Romans 6:23

The wages of sin is death, but the gift of God is eternal life through Jesus Christ.

Romans 6:23

What do you think of when you hear the word *curve*? If you're a baseball fan, it's a nasty breaking ball that buckles the batter's knees before diving over the inside corner for called strike three, the twelve o'clock to six o'clock curve ball that literally falls off a table. If you are a road-racing fan, it could remind you of Dead Man's Curve, where a driver is precariously close to the Baja cliff, tires squealing and gravel flying to maintain traction. Kids in school hope for the bell curve to keep from flunking a test and keep their hopes alive for the college of their choice. If students are fortunate, they'll get a teacher who grades on the bell curve, a teacher who gives so many As, so many Bs, and so many Cs. Even though you might do poorly on a test and never demonstrate that you knew the material, you will get that A if you have one of the highest scores. If I'm better than most, I will get my reward. But when a teacher doesn't use the bell curve, students and parents are outraged. The parents scream, "It's not fair that you are keeping our child from getting into UGA!"

Well, guess what? When it comes to God's expectations of us and the way he judges us, he doesn't use a bell-shaped curve and never will. God is strictly pass/fail. Many people believe that they will make the cut and go to heaven simply because, "I'm not a murderer or rapist, and I don't do drugs or drink alcohol or have premarital sex. Many of my classmates do, so surely I will go to heaven instead of them." That's not the message of the Bible through the Ten Commandments. The Bible makes it clear that sin is sin, no matter how large or small, whether it is action or simply a thought. Roaming eyes and adultery are sinful, hatred of another person and murder are sinful, and putting yourself first ahead of God and others is idolatry. Romans 6:23 reminds us that the wages of sin is death. Sin is the breaking of any of God's rules in the Bible, not just the bad sins. Any sin results in spiritual death unless you repent and know Jesus and Jesus knows you.

God's final has the following two questions: 1) Have you repented of all your sins? 2) Have you placed your trust in Christ? The answers to those two questions are solely determined by you and will determine your home for eternity.

Prayer: Father God, may I never believe that I can get to heaven by being good enough or better than somebody else. I know that it is only by the cross of Calvary that I will ever be with you. In Jesus's name, amen.

BB06:
BLOCKBUSTER TRADE

2 Corinthians 5:17–20

He is not the same anymore, a new life has begun!

2 Corinthians 5:17

Professional teams swap or trade players in hopes of improving their teams. A trade can wind up helping both teams, or one team might be helped greatly and the other team is hurt tremendously. A trade that yields a huge potential change in a team's immediate future or swaps very important players is called a blockbuster trade.

In 1920, the Boston Red Sox, after winning two world championships, traded a promising left-handed pitcher to the New York Yankees. The Yankees had been the weaker of the two teams, but the trade immediately enhanced their club. In fact, it changed the fortunes of both franchises forever and triggered one of the most intense rivalries in sports. The Yankees recognized the power hitting ability of their new player and moved him to right field so that he could play every day. He hit third in the lineup and wore number three. His name was George Herman "Babe" Ruth, who became known as the Sultan of Swat for his prodigious home runs. He hit 714 of them, and Babe led the Yankees to many world championships.

The Red Sox suffered almost ninety years of heartache, often at the hands of the Yankees, before an improbable 0–3 playoff series comeback against the Yankees in 2004. The Red Sox finally won the World Series and overcame what was known as The Curse of the Bambino.

You can make a blockbuster trade that will hurt Satan's team and help God's team. That trade occurs when you decide to trade or exchange your sinful, selfish life for a new life in Jesus Christ. Babe Ruth put on a new uniform and began a new career in right field batting third. You can put on your new life when you repent of or turn from all your sins in godly sorrow with the commitment to leave those sins behind you. When you repent, you are cleansed by the blood shed for you by Jesus Christ. When you ask Jesus to come into your heart because you believe that he died for your sins, you immediately receive God's grace and the free gift of eternal life. When you exchange Satan's team for God's team, that's one blockbuster trade for the ages.

You can never be traded back either. You don't need an owner or general manager or coach or even a mom or dad to initiate the trade. You can do it yourself. You've wanted to do other things by yourself for your entire life without anybody's help, and here is your chance. No matter how old you are or where you live, won't you invite Christ to give you a brand-new life? The Bible assures you, "When you become a Christian, you are a new person inside. You are not the same anymore, a new life has begun!" (2 Corinthians 5:17). There is no fresh start like a new life on God's team.

Prayer: Father God, thank you that I can choose to immediately exchange my sinful life for a new life in Christ. Lord, I trust that you will do the changing and transforming after I make this blockbuster trade. In Jesus's name, amen.

BB07:
WHO AM I TO JUDGE?

Job 38, Matthew 7:1–5

Where were you when I laid the foundations of the earth?

Job 38:4

Baseball teams create media guides that contain player profiles. The profile gives you very limited information about the player, sort of a thumbnail sketch. The profile will give you the player's full name, age, left-handed or right-handed batter, height, weight, and stats for the current year and previous years. There could be some personal information such as the player's wife and kids, residence, and fun facts such as favorite food, musician, and activity. The FCA magazine *Sharing the Victory* provides quotes from the player about his or her Christian walk and a favorite verse of Scripture.

But what we know about a player is far less than what we don't know. I'm sure that you've heard the saying "the tip of the iceberg." What lies above the surface is vastly different than what lies below the surface. So little is known about the entire iceberg, and so little is known about all of the circumstances that shaped a player's life.

We see a person's outward manifestations of character and his reactions in certain situations. Then we become judge of the universe (God) and criticize the person. Of course, it is a sin to judge the person because we've made ourselves God, which dings the first two commandments. We are guilty of judging another person's intentions when we know so little about the situation. We hear one remark or see a person dressed in a different fashion and immediately our mind makes them out to be a bad person.

Just as we know very little about the circumstances that shaped a player's life, Job knew a lot less than God did about the reasons for his circumstances. When Job questioned God regarding the circumstances of his dire situation, implying that he knew enough to challenge God about his situation or that God had made a mistake, God broke his silence with Job. God unleashed a torrent of questions, reminding Job that he is the Maker and Master of all and that Job should let God do the judging. God had so much more knowledge than Job, just as he has so much more knowledge about situations than we do. My knowledge compared to God's knowledge is but a grain of sand in the Sahara Desert. God is all knowing, all present, and in everything. There are literally thousands of situations and experiences that shape a person's actions. God knows them all, and we don't. Who was, is, and always will be in the best place to judge? God. Before you judge another person, look for the speck in your left eye and the log in your right eye.

Prayer: Dear heavenly Father, please forgive me when I am so quick to play God by taking the first morsel of information and attempting to paint the whole picture. Only you are omnipotent, omniscient, and omnipresent. You are timeless and present in billions of places, and I can only be in one place at one time. When I take that incomplete information and judge a person, please show me my sinful action through the Holy Spirit. May I leave the judging to you. In Jesus's holy name, I pray. Amen.

BB08:
JUST WHO ARE YOU
TRYING TO IMPRESS?

Matthew 16:26, Mark 8:34–38

For what profit is it to a man if he gains the whole world and loses his soul? And what will a man give in exchange for his own soul?

Matthew 16:26

In the fifth grade, I became best friends with Mickey and Mike at my new school in Rentz. The three of us were already huge sports fans, and we would try to impress each other with our sports knowledge and try to one up each other. One morning, when I arrived at school, I knew that I had them. The previous night, I climbed into bed and put my transistor AM radio under my pillow. I carefully turned on the radio so that it didn't pop with static and wake up my mother. I tuned the radio to 700 WLW in Cincinnati to pick up the Reds-Dodgers game. But the game started when it was 11:00 P.M. in Cadwell, Georgia. Sandy Koufax pitched for the Dodgers, which usually meant a two-hour game because he was the top pitcher in baseball. However, the game was tied 1–1 after nine innings. Finally, the Reds won 3–1 in thirteen innings. The clock read 3:00 A.M. Mickey and Mike were appropriately wowed at recess the next morning as I proudly boasted of my exploits that went undetected by my parents.

Now here is the question. Who the heck was I trying to impress? So many times, I have wasted time and energy to accomplish firsts for which there is no eternal benefit. When life comes to a close, I'm pretty sure that I will wish that I had spent more time on items of eternal significance and less time getting my golf handicap down. You know the line that you cross when the final score matters way too much. As you delve into another meaningless, trivial project of minutiae, or one more stint on the blogs, ask yourself if the effort is of eternal significance. If the answer is no, evaluate the time and energy that you're devoting. You and I are better off getting a little extra sleep.

Prayer: Father God, help me direct my time and energy to activities that are for your glory and not mine. May I recognize quickly when I have crossed the line that is all about my glory and not yours. In Jesus's name, amen.

BB09: JEFF FRANCOEUR

Joshua 1:9

Have I not commanded you? Be strong and courageous. Do not be terrified; do not be discouraged, for the LORD your God will be with you wherever you go.

Jeff Francoeur was one of the most famous high school stars in Georgia at Parkview High School, leading the Panthers to football and state baseball championships when he was a senior. Jeff signed with the Atlanta Braves and spent several years in the minor leagues. In Double AA ball, Jeff was struck in the face with a 95-mile-per-hour fastball and missed five weeks of the season. To encourage him in his recovery, Jeff's mother recited a verse, Joshua 1:9, to him every day to help him overcome his setback.

One year later, in July 2005, he burst onto the major league scene by hitting .400 during his first month with the Atlanta Braves. He electrified crowds with his home runs, great catches, and sensational throws that gunned down runners at the plate. He made the USA World Baseball Team even though he was only a rookie. Jeff graced the cover of Sports Illustrated with the caption of "The Natural." But Jeff was glorifying in himself after his great start instead of giving God the credit.

At the start of the 2006 season, he went into a 2-for-32 slump that made him hit rock bottom. He then realized that he needed to give

God all the glory and trust in him completely. Jeff confessed to God that he had given him only 80 percent of his heart and that he had held onto the other 20 percent for baseball. Relying on the skills of "The Natural" was insufficient, Jeff realized. It was at that moment that Jeff committed his whole heart, 100 percent of it, to God.

Prayer: Heavenly Father, thank you for the lesson that Jeff learned that he could not do baseball on his own. Help me remember that apart from you, I can do nothing. Yet everything is possible when I work through you and not around you. In the precious name of our Lord, amen.

BB10:
ALBERT PUJOLS

John 14:6

I am The Way, The Truth, and The Life. No one comes to the Father except through me.

Albert Pujols, a first baseman with the St. Louis Cardinals, is recognized as perhaps the best player in the game. He is hitting .329 with over 400 home runs during eleven brilliant major-league seasons and has become a Gold Glove-caliber fielder. But the humility of this Dominican Republic native is readily apparent.

Even though he's been in America a long time, it took him years to feel comfortable addressing crowds. Albert and his wife, Deidre, have been involved in Christian Family Days in St. Louis. In the past, Pujols would simply come out and wave to the crowd.

But Pujols spoke these words after the 2007 St. Louis Cardinal Christian Family Day event:

> Just because I've got God in my heart and I'm a great baseball player, that doesn't mean that I'm perfect. I'm just a human person just like everybody else here, and I make mistakes. Only God was perfect. He's obviously using me by giving me this platform so I can honor him and get to know more people and just share the gospel with those who need [it].

Albert's reluctance to speak reminds us of Moses. When it was time to lead God's people out of Egypt, Moses told God that he was not an eloquent speaker by any stretch of the imagination. But God assured Moses that he would be with him and teach him what to say. When we are uncomfortable about speaking to a group, remember that God is always there to help us if we will only reach out to him.

Prayer: Father God, help me learn from the grace and humility of Albert Pujols. May I realize that I'm going to make errors today, and that your perfect love, mercy, and grace will restore me when I confess those failures to you. In Jesus's name, amen.

BB11:
JOHN SMOLTZ

James 2:17

Faith, if not accompanied by action, is dead.

John Smoltz holds one of the most unique records in the history of baseball. He was a star pitcher with the Atlanta Braves and was the first major-league pitcher ever to post 200 wins and 200 saves. Smoltz is also remembered by fans as one of the top post-season pitchers ever.

In 1995, one evening, as he was eating dinner with the team chaplain, John posed some questions he had about becoming a Christian.

"I asked him this question. I said, 'I've prayed the prayer. [It] keeps me from living my life the way I want to live it. [At age forty-five or forty-six], I'll turn it over to the Lord, and the rest will be history. What prevents me from doing that?' He simply looked at me and said, 'Nothing prevents you from doing that with just one tiny exception. You might not make your target date. You are not in control of your next breath.'

"My rules were I played for me," says Smoltz. "Now, it's a different set of rules so that God gets all the glory. I am as competitive as the next person, but I don't go to the extreme. I try to live my life so that if no one ever hears me say a word, they watch me and judge me by my actions. If you never heard me say a word, you would say 'There's something special about that guy—he's different.'"

John's experiences remind us that as long as we play for ourselves first instead of Christ, praying a prayer of confession may not result in a changed life. But when we decide to put God first once and for all and give him the glory, our actions begin to reveal the living Christ within us to our friends.

Prayer: Father God, help me to live my life in a way that the people that I meet will be attracted to the presence of Christ in me. May I realize that God gives us today to make a difference in his kingdom. In Jesus's name, amen.

BB12:
ARE YOU JUST GUESSING?

John 14:6

I am The Way, The Truth, and The Life. No one comes to the Father except through me.

As my elderly dad persevered through the first few years after my mother passed away, he began to watch the Andy Griffith DVD series daily. Thanks to my niece, he has every Andy Griffith show ever filmed, all eight seasons. The DVDs give him much-needed entertainment and help him pass some time each day. For a while, he would watch the first few innings of Atlanta Braves games before bedtime, so I could talk to him about baseball. One year, I went to see him just before the All-Star game. He asked how many Braves had made the All-Star team. I commented that two Braves had been named to the team: John Smoltz and Tom Glavine. Then I added the names of several other players but wound up retracting one name, which made my answer highly questionable. I didn't know for sure which Braves had made the team. Dad recognized my uncertainty and said rather succinctly, "Do you know, or are you guessing?" I admitted that I was guessing.

My girls and I have laughed about that line and have re-used it to tease each other. However, one decision you don't want to be guessing about is your salvation. "Do you know you are saved, or are you guessing?" That is one question of which you need to be 100 percent sure. If Jesus lives in your heart, we know it because the Holy Spirit keeps us focused on things other than ourselves. Sometimes the cares of the world can make us lose our focus on God, but then we bounce back through God's power and the Holy Spirit living within us. It's also evident by the fruit that we bear for Christ in living our daily lives. Another sign is that things that were once important to us no longer have the same relevance.

If you have never been sure of your salvation in Christ, the stakes are too high to be wondering. You can guess which stocks will rise, or what your tire pressure is, or who your favorite team's next head football coach will be, but be sure of your salvation.

Prayer: Most gracious God, thank you for the godly confidence that you give me as a Christian to know that I have been born again through your free gift of grace. If I'm not sure, I want to be sure. I want to know you and I want to get to heaven. I'm sorry for my sin that you had to die for, and I ask you to save me now. Jesus, I believe you are the only way to the Father. In Jesus's name, amen.

BB13:
COME OUT AND PLAY WITH ME

1 Corinthians 9:22, Revelation 3:20

Behold, I stand at the door and knock...

Revelation 3:20

One of the joys of my childhood was when one of my two best friends would knock on my front door and say, "Come out and play with me!" My best friends were Darryl and Joel. When Darryl came over, sometimes we threw the baseball, rode our bicycles, or went to the community pool. When Joel came over, we would most always play baseball against the side of my house. We would pretend that we played for professional baseball teams. I would pick the Braves, and Joel would pick the Reds and load his lineup with right-handed batters. He would pitch to the strike zone that we drew on the chimney, and I would hit, and vice versa. The pitcher would announce the game, and we would play a regulation nine-inning game in about two hours. We made up many ground rules. A ball hit over the pear tree was a home run, and a ball hit between two stones that were about three feet apart was a double. We played for hours until we came inside for snacks and cold lemonade. Obviously, it wouldn't have been nearly as much fun to stay inside the house during the day and play Monopoly. The real fun was outside.

One of the joys and responsibilities of being a Christian was described by Kennon Callahan in his book *Twelve Keys to an Effective Church*. Dr. Callahan pointed out that the Revelation 3:20 verse is most often described as the verse where Jesus comes into your heart. "Behold, I stand at the door and knock. If anyone hears my voice and opens the door, I will come into Him and dine with Him, and Him with me." Pretend there is a door into your heart. There's no doorknob on the outside door, so you must open the door from the inside to allow Jesus to come in. Jesus will never force his way in.

Dr. Callahan pointed out that as Christians we are also supposed to step outside into the mission field after Jesus comes into our hearts. Just as my friends invited me to come out and play, Jesus invites us to come out and play with him in the mission field. We are called to go out into the mission field, either globally or locally, by the Great Commission (Matthew 28:19–20). You've probably seen this sign when you leave some churches: "You are entering the mission field." Whether we leave church or our house in the morning, let's realize that we are entering the mission field at work, at school, or at play.

Feel ill equipped to come outside to play with Jesus? Remember how you were better at some games than others. You were a pretty good hitter right-handed, but you couldn't hit a lick left-handed. When God creates us, he gives us special talents and a passion that are unlike other people's. If you tap into God's plan for your life, you will be fired up to go out into the mission field. But he doesn't want you out there as a left-hander if you are right-handed. I barely know a hammer from a chisel, so God doesn't expect me to project manage Habitat for Humanity builds. I would be miserable. My passion is helping young people play sports in a gym and using those opportunities to teach them about Jesus Christ. As Paul taught us, he tried to meet people where they were so they would let him tell them about Christ and let God do the rest. God wants to meet you where your passion lies.

Prayer: Father God, give me the heart and desire to come outside and play in one of your mission fields. Help me discover that the Christian walk is a lot more fun and beneficial to God's kingdom when I serve in an area that you made me really good at. May I know that you and the Holy Spirit will help me use that passion to shine my light so that others can see and experience your mighty love. In Jesus's most holy and precious name, amen.

BB14:
MOUTH OF THE SOUTH

Matthew 12:34, James 1:26, 1 Peter 5:7

Out of the overflow of the heart, the mouth speaks.

Matthew 12:34

When I was a kid, I had a pretty good mouth on me. Besides learning how to cuss with the best of them, my smart mouth got me into trouble from time to time. Plus, you surely didn't want to be around me when I missed a shot on the golf course.

Once, I smarted off to my mother, and she drew her hand back and swatted me on the butt. I saw it coming and lurched forward, and her hand struck me on the tailbone. She started crying because it hurt her hand, and I remember thinking, *Good! Because that makes two of us who are hurting.*

Dad coached the high school baseball team at Laurens High. Our biggest rival was Dexter, and we played at Dexter one afternoon. Their umpire was a good friend of my sister, who taught at the school and lived in Dexter with her husband. Mr. Kitchens called strike three on our batter on a pitch that I thought was outside. I was about twelve when I yelled, "There's some home cooking!" You could just see the man's neck turn bright red with anger and embarrassment. I was showing off and trying to draw attention, not thinking how I could hurt someone's feelings.

Later that season, Laurens High hosted the region baseball tournament. I enjoyed helping Dad get the field ready each day, and he let me be the official scorekeeper for the tournament. The championship game pitted Mount de Sales against Dexter. Late in the game, a Mount de Sales player hit a double that cleared the bases and should have locked up the game. But no. Mr. Big Mouth declared to all who were sitting near him in the bleachers that a runner had missed third base. A Dexter fan yelled, "Throw it to third! He missed the base." Dexter threw the ball to third, and sure enough, the umpire rang up the third out of the inning. A shudder went through me, and I could feel the icy stare of the de Sales nuns on my neck.

These stories are of a young man who did not know Christ. I look back at my friend, Thomas, who knew Jesus. I don't recall seeing this type of behavior out of him. He knew how to have fun, laugh, and joke, but it wasn't at someone else's expense.

The books of James and Matthew make it clear that the thoughts in the heart will overflow to the mouth. When I came to know Jesus, it was suddenly as if God had placed a delay mechanism into my brain that gave me an extra couple of seconds to think. Sure, I can still get angry and say the wrong things, especially when I'm tired and it's late, but it doesn't happen nearly so often and never profanely. Curbing my anger and profane outbursts was a little miracle that God worked in my life that lets me know that I truly know Jesus as my Savior and Lord. That delay mechanism living in me? It must be the Holy Spirit.

Any believer will slip from time to time. An outburst can happen when we are under pressure, and it hurts our witness in the world. We can talk to God about the pressures, strains, and stresses of everyday life. God already knows what is bothering us, but he wants to hear from us anyway. God "watches everything that concerns us and is always thinking about us" (1 Peter 5:7). Release your frustrations, anger, and hurts to the same Father who wonderfully and fearfully made you.

Prayer: Father God, thank you for the special touch, which is yours and yours alone, that changes angry hearts and gives us the peace that passes understanding. In the holy name of Jesus, amen.

BB15:
BASEBALL'S STAR

Jeremiah 29:11, Romans 5:8, 1 John 1:9,
John 3:16, Ephesians 2:8

For God so loved the world that He gave his only begotten Son, that whosoever believes in Him shall not perish but have everlasting life.

John 3:16

Willie Mays was one of the greatest stars in the history of baseball because he could do five things well. First, he could hit for average. Second, he could steal bases. Third, he could hit for power or home runs. Fourth, he had one of the greatest throwing arms ever. Fifth, he could play defense like few center fielders before or since, chasing down seemingly uncatchable balls with his cap flying off.

Just as I listed five reasons that Willie Mays was a great baseball player, one for each point on a star, there are five points that every person needs to understand about salvation. The first point is that you are wonderfully and uniquely made (Psalm 139:14) by God, and there is no one else quite like you. God created a unique life plan (Jeremiah 29:11) just for you, his special child whom he loves perfectly.

The second point is that each person is separated from God when he or she consciously breaks one of God's rules that are called the Ten Commandments. Each person inherits a sinful nature at birth (Psalm

51:5) and is destined to commit sin as a child. Everyone has experienced separation from God due to sin (Romans 3:23), and we must address it, or spiritual death (Romans 6:23) will be the end result.

Point number three is that God loved us so much in spite of our shortcomings that even while we were sinners (Romans 5:8), he sent Jesus to pay the price for the sin that threatens to separate us from God permanently. Jesus even carried our sin in his body to the cross (1 Peter 2:24). But believers celebrate every day that Jesus left the tomb and came back to life (Matthew 28:6).

God took care of the first three points. The next two points are up to us. The fourth point is that you must make the commitment to exchange your sinful life for a new life in Christ. You must repent, or turn away from your sinful life and turn toward God, asking him to forgive you (1 John 1:9) and to cleanse you of all your sin (1 John 1:7).

The fifth point is that you must trust and accept God's gift of grace to receive eternal life (Ephesians 2:8), admitting that you cannot earn God's grace and that salvation only comes through his Son, Jesus Christ (John 3:16). Commit to obey God daily by praying and studying his Word to grow in Christ in all aspects of your life (Proverbs 3:6).

God offers everyone his free gift of grace. I invite you to pray this prayer to receive Jesus Christ into your life as your Savior. Your attitude and change of heart is more important than these exact words.

Prayer: "Most holy and precious Jesus, I need you. Thank you for suffering on the cross and dying for my sins. I want my life to change. Please forgive all of my sins through your blood that flowed so freely for me. Jesus, come into my heart. Thank you for your free gift of grace that brings me eternal life in heaven. Thank you for accepting me as a child of God. In Jesus's holy name, I pray. Amen."

BB16:
YOUR SIN IS FORGIVEN NO MATTER HOW GRIEVOUS

Hebrews 10:17

I will never again remember their sins and lawless deeds.

There is a great scene from the baseball movie *Fever Pitch*. Jimmy Fallon stars as Ben, the obsessed Red Sox fan. His Red Sox friends are explaining the Curse of the Bambino and the various failures of the Red Sox over the past ninety years to his new girlfriend. One of them simply says, "Buckner," and they all groan and turn away.

Bill Buckner was one of the more consistent hitters in baseball history and played for the world champion Dodgers before signing with the Red Sox. In the tenth inning of game six of the 1986 World Series, while playing first base on two sprained ankles, Buckner allowed a ground ball to go through his legs. If he had fielded it properly, Buckner could have helped Boston win its first World Series title in almost seventy years. As a result of one unfortunate play, he was ostracized by Red Sox fans. He received death threats and, obviously, many Bosox fans bashed him for years. Hopefully some of those fans felt pangs of regret after the Sox won the World Series in 2004 after a miracle comeback against the Yankees in the ALCS.

No matter what grievous sin you have committed, God will forgive you when you earnestly repent, and he won't hold out on you for years. You will receive immediate forgiveness. Here is what is really amazing and cool. When God forgives, God forgets, like it never happened. God will, in essence, say, "I don't remember any missed ground ball. You are forgiven."

Prayer: Father God, thank you in advance for forgiving any of the vast array of sins that I am capable of committing. I am blown away that you will forgive and forget my sin. You are so good and so wonderful and bless me in so many ways. In the precious name of Jesus, amen.

BB17:
ALIGN YOUR TRADEMARK WITH GOD'S PLAN

Jeremiah 29:11, 13

I know the plans I have for you, says the Lord, plans for welfare and not for harm, to give you a future with hope… You shall find the Lord when you seek Him with your whole heart.

The Hillerich and Bradsby Co. in Louisville, Kentucky, has been the most famous baseball bat maker in America for about a century. In its heyday, H&B made millions of wooden bats per year. In each bat, the workers burn the well-known "Louisville Slugger" trademark into the middle of the bat across the wood grain. Here is why that detail is so important.

One of the first things I learned as a boy was to hold the trademark at a 90-degree angle from the pitcher so that the trademark faced the dugout. The reason is that bats break when you hit the ball on the trademark, and they are very expensive to replace. Most Little League, high school, and college teams use metal bats because of the replacement expense and the extra pop that metal bats provide. But occasionally, there are some wood bat tournaments when this generation of boys experiences what it felt like to get "good wood on it."

If you don't align the trademark of the bat properly, a mishit will cause the bat to break. Today, it is commonplace to see a bat shatter into pieces because the players want so much of the overall weight of the bat in the barrel. The barrel will fly into the infield, and the shortstop ducks to avoid the bat and still catch the ball. If you hit the ball on the handle on a cold day, not only will your bat break but your hands will sting from the vibration.

Align your life with God or face the stinging consequences of sin. You might even feel the shattering results of bad decisions. Don't let it happen to you. Connect with God's plan for your life by studying his Word and through prayer and meditation. By staying close to God, you will align your trademark with God, avoid the sting and bitterness of defeat, and relish in the joy of being flush in the Lord with his plan for your life.

Prayer: Oh, Lord, I really want to align my plans with your plan for my life. Help me see the pitfalls and avoid them so that I can be fully tapped into your power and holiness. In Jesus's name, amen.

BB18:
MY LONGEST DAY UMPIRING

Psalm 121:1–2

I lift my eyes unto the hills, where does my help come from?
My help comes from the Lord, maker of Heaven and earth.

I began umpiring Little League games during my summers when I was home from college. At the University of Georgia, I joined the local high school baseball umpires association and managed to work a couple of years of high school games in the Athens area. After I graduated from UGA and lived at home for a year, I started a year-round recreation program in Laurens County. During the spring, I had free time, so I continued my umpiring. I had developed a pretty good strike zone and mechanics, so the head of the association assigned me to a college scrimmage. It went really well, and I felt like I missed only two or three pitches during the game. Before I knew it, there I was, only twenty-three years old, working a ten-game junior college schedule. Pretty heady stuff.

I was assigned to work the games with Reuben Dawson, an old codger, a veteran ump. He would work the first game of the double-header behind the plate, and I would work the second game. The first three doubleheaders went fine, but the next one was a disaster. I'll never forget the coach, Clyde Miller. I started off a little shaky behind the plate, and he spied it like a shark seeing blood in the water. Faint blood, but blood nonetheless. During the second inning, he argued with my ball-strike calls and challenged my manhood. I completely lost my command of the strike zone and made some terrible calls. I had never felt so defeated and embarrassed.

It's been over thirty-five years, and I can still see him go up one side and down the other, giving me you know what. It was by far my most exasperating day on the baseball diamond. I opted out of the final doubleheader of the season and never called another high school or college game.

Jesus Christ knows exactly how we feel, no matter the disappointment or the pain. God sent his Son to live among us so that he would feel any emotion that we could possibly feel. Through Christ, we can find solace and strength in the midst of our disappointments and failures. I wish that I had known Christ at the time so that I could have shared my sorrow with the Man of Sorrows.

Prayer: Father God, you are so loving and want the best for me. When I hang my head, remind me that I am a child of God, I am safe in your arms, and that no matter how badly I perform, you will never leave me nor forsake me. In Jesus's name, amen.

BB19:
LITTLE LEAGUE WORLD SERIES

John 14:6

I am The Way, The Truth, and the Life. No one comes to the Father except through me.

Each summer, several million boys and thousands of girls around the world try to qualify for the Little League World Series in Williamsport, Pennsylvania. There is now a similar tournament for girls' softball. There are only sixteen teams that make it to Williamsport, eight from the United States, and eight from the rest of the world. The players are treated like royalty by the people of the town. The players get to play on international TV. When they come to bat, the profiles of their favorite foods, athletes, and TV shows are flashed on the screen. This tournament will be the most exciting week in the lives of many of these eleven, twelve, and thirteen-year-olds.

As a young boy, my summer days revolved around the games that I would play in Dublin, Georgia. I had so many great times and experiences. I made the All-Star team of ten through twelve boys four years in a row beginning at the age of nine. I was the second alternate on the team. When two boys chose not to play, I was officially pulled onto the team. I will never forget what a thrill it was to sit between the top two twelve-year-old stars on the bus ride to Warner Robins. I thought that I was pretty big stuff. In fact, being an All-Star gave me a pretty inflated view of myself. I was Danny Farr, All-Star, as if it was part of my name.

When I was eleven, our team won the state championship and finished third when I was twelve. I have often said that those experiences were the highlight of my childhood. But my ultimate highlight during that period could have been a decision to know Jesus Christ when I was moved by the Holy Spirit, but I choked back the decision. *Next week, I'll come forward,* I surmised, but my decision to receive Christ didn't happen for another thirty-five years.

These eleven, twelve, and thirteen-year-olds are at such an impressionable age. This group needs positive reinforcement for their psyches. I could never have imagined playing in front of forty thousand people as these boys do at the Little League World Series. For those who experience the thrill of the Little League World Series, may it be surpassed one day with the joy of knowing Jesus Christ as Savior and Lord.

Prayer: Father God, help me see how to reach impressionable young people with the knowledge of your saving grace. It will only get tougher to come to Jesus as they get older. May they come to know Christ at an early age. In Jesus's name, amen.

BB20:
MEN OF COURAGE

Galatians 3:24–29

There is neither Jew nor Greek, there is neither slave nor free, there is neither male nor female: for you are all one in Christ Jesus.

Galatians 3:28

Jackie Robinson is perhaps the most revered baseball player in history because he was able to break through the color barrier that had existed in major league baseball for the better part of a century. An All-American running back at UCLA, Jackie was a tremendous package of strength, speed, agility, and, most of all, true grit. He had a very successful career, and ever since, players of all colors have paid tribute to the courage that he displayed. By overcoming adversity Jackie not only opened the door for African Americans but also for players from the Dominican Republic and other countries.

It also took courage from another man to make the Jackie Robinson story become a reality. No baseball owner had ever signed an African American. Branch Rickey of the Brooklyn Dodgers signed Jackie Robinson of UCLA in 1947 to a contract after careful deliberation that this young man had what it took. After all, a failure by the first African American to withstand the pressure of derogatory statements could set back the integration of baseball for many years. The

Robinson signing was a precursor of things to come, as Rosa Parks became the first African American to ride in the front of the bus in Montgomery, Alabama.

Branch Rickey was a man of strong Christian beliefs and believed that it was wrong to exclude persons because of their race. When Jackie Robinson is mentioned, it should also be noted that it took someone of courage to give him that opportunity. Baseball and other major sports have never been the same, as all people have been given opportunity to entertain us with their tremendous skills.

Why did it take America so long to come to its senses, over eighty years after the Civil War? I cannot explain it, but one thing is for sure. Paul echoed the teachings of Jesus that all should be treated equally and have an opportunity to come to Christ. The poor, the oppressed, the bound, and the women did not have rights in Jesus's time either. Christ's message of love and acceptance changed the world when Christ walked among us, and the promise of hope for the oppressed continues to change the world today.

Prayer: Most high God, thank you for the courage of the man who made the game-changing decision and for the courage of the man who took advantage of the game-changing decision that opened the door for minorities all over the world. It is so wonderful that Branch Rickey chose to align with the teachings of Jesus and Paul. In Jesus's name, amen.

BB21:
HANK AARON 715

Joshua 1:9

Have I not commanded you? Do not be afraid, do not be dismayed. For the Lord your God is with you wherever you go.

On April 8, 1974, Hank Aaron of the Atlanta Braves broke baseball's most hallowed record: Babe Ruth's 714 home runs. In the months leading up to this incredible accomplishment, he received hundreds of pieces of hate mail and death threats because of the color of his skin. Through it all, Aaron showed a remarkable sense of calm. He weathered many storms to be able to hang in there and get the record.

We weathered a storm in Macon to get to the game. Before the season started, I ordered six tickets to opening day. My friend, Joel, my brother, L. E., and his wife, Gail, my sister, Regina, and her husband, Bennie, and I set sail for Atlanta with the hopes of seeing baseball's most immortal record broken. As we approached Macon, the skies darkened and the wind howled. We were driving in Regina and Bennie's brand-new Chevrolet sedan, and the weather became so fierce on I-16 that we pulled onto the right of way. Suddenly, hail as big as marbles pelted our car and left many tiny dents all over their brand-new car. After the storm passed, we took a quick opinion poll and agreed that if the weather was that bad on the other side of Macon, we weren't going to the game. But the skies cleared, the sun came out, and we headed to Atlanta. Man, would I have kicked myself if I had missed seeing the greatest record in the history of baseball fall.

All of us can take solace and encouragement from the words of Joshua, who encouraged us to not be afraid and to not be dismayed, for God is with us wherever we go. God was there for Hank Aaron to give him the courage to face adversity and danger, and he is with us to give us the same strength and protection no matter what we're facing. God is so good all the time. All the time, God is good.

Prayer: Father God, in this time, when so many athletes seem to be shirking their opportunities to be role models for this generation, thank you for the lasting legacy of Henry "Hank" Aaron. I thank you for his gracious demeanor that was only exceeded by his iron will to succeed. In Jesus's name, amen.

BB22:
PRACTICE MAKES PERFECT

Philippians 1:6

Being confident of this very thing, that He who has begun a new work in you will complete it until the day of Jesus Christ.

My brother, L. E., coached my Little League team in the summer, and he would practice us several hours per day in the middle of the hot day. L. E. played shortstop on his college team at the time, so he had quite an arm. He would pitch rubber balls as fast as he could to improve our bat speed. He would cut the rubber balls in half and throw us wicked curve balls. If we could hit these pitches in practice, we could certainly hit the pitches thrown to us by eleven and twelve-year-olds. He would hit many ground balls, and Thomas and I would practice turning the double play again and again.

He gave us plenty of hitting and fielding practice to help us grow as players. If we simply showed up at our games without this intense practice, we wouldn't have played nearly as well. When I was eleven, our team from the little town of Cadwell placed six players in the starting lineup of our county All-Star team, which won the Georgia parks and recreation state title.

If we expect to grow as Christians, we can't just come to church once a week or every couple of weeks and expect to grow in our faith. Daily practice through prayer, meditation, Bible reading, and devotions will all help us grow effectively as Christians. With steady diligence, our obedience and love for God will grow. We will still commit errors (sins), but they should become fewer and farther between. Eventually, when we meet Christ one glorious day, he will make us perfect.

Prayer: Father God, may I use the lessons learned from my experiences to become a more ardent follower. I need to practice daily through reading the Word, meditation, and prayer. In Jesus's name, amen.

BB23:
FOUL BALLS IN THE STANDS

Habakkuk 3:18–19

Yes I will rejoice in the Lord. I will joy in the God of my salvation. The Lord God is my strength ...

Ever notice how the fans in major league ball parks react when a foul ball flies into the stands? People of all ages will scramble for the prize souvenir and will do whatever it takes to come up with the ball. But once someone has secured the ball, a pretty cool thing happens. All the people in the immediate areas are smiling and laughing from the thrill of being part of the game.

The exception is if someone gets drilled with the baseball, which is never a good thing. Remember when Ben's girlfriend in *Fever Pitch* got drilled with the foul ball and wound up with a bag of frozen peas on her forehead?

But so long as no one gets hit with the ball, folks will be laughing and smiling, and somebody comes away with the great thrill of a major league souvenir.

How long has it been since you've relaxed enough to have a good belly laugh? Laughter is truly a gift from God, especially when we laugh with people and not at them. If you haven't had a good laugh in way too long, find a humorous friend or a funny book or movie. Laughter is the best medicine.

Prayer: Father God, thank you for blessing me with the wonderful sense of laughter that helps me get through some tough times. Laughter is a great way for me to shine the light of your love. Please give me opportunities today to laugh and love. In Jesus's name, amen.

BB24:
HERE COMES THE THROW!
HE IS ...SAFE!

Romans 10:8–13

That if you confess with your mouth the Lord Jesus, and shall believe in your heart that God has raised him from the dead, you shall be saved.

Romans 10:9

Atlanta Braves first baseman Sid Bream carefully inched off second base. The 1992 National League Championship Series between the Braves and the Pittsburgh Pirates was tied at three games apiece, and the Braves were down 2–1 with the bases loaded and two out in the bottom of the ninth inning. Atlanta Fulton County Stadium was in an uproar as pinch-hitter Francisco Cabrera came to the plate to win it or lose the series for the Braves. As the clock approached midnight, he cracked a hit to left field.

Despite his cumbersome knee brace and lumbering gait, Bream charged around third and sprinted for home. With a determined slide, Sid barely beat the throw, which was slightly up the first-base side. Bream was safe as the late Skip Caray screamed, "He is ...safe! Braves win! Braves win! Braves win!" Sid's teammates piled on top of him and each other at home plate as the city of Atlanta exploded with joy.

My daughters, Allison and Jillian, still enjoy reminding me that after Bream was called safe at the plate, I ran out our front door and screamed my version of "Braves win! Braves win! Braves win!" for the neighborhood. They were eight and five at the time, so you might say that my antics left an indelible impression.

Sid Bream had a successful baseball career, but he developed major health problems soon after his career ended. I came to find out from researching his sickness that Sid was a believer. Here is an excerpt that I pulled from Sid's bio on a Christian speakers' website.

"Sid had many memorable moments, but the one that meant the most was sliding home in the 1992 National League Championship Series against the Pittsburgh Pirates in the seventh game. Sid is an avid outdoorsman and loves to talk about God's awesome handprint across this world. Today, after baseball, Sid spends most of his time speaking in churches, youth groups, and schools all over America."

You never know the background of some ballplayers or people with whom we come in contact. No matter the outcome of his health problems, he would be forever safe for eternity with the Lord. Right now, would you be called safe in the Lord for eternity or called out?

Prayer: Most gracious God, I thank you that when I get to the pearly gates, I will be called safe and allowed to enter because of your free gift of grace. I pray those reading this devotion will be called safe also. In Jesus's name, amen.

BB25:
LET'S PLAY TWO

Colossians 3:23

Work hard and cheerfully at all you do, just as though you were working for your Lord and not just for your masters.

Ernie Banks of the Chicago Cubs remains one of the most popular sports figures to play in the Windy City. He was so popular and such a great representative of the Cubs organization that he was affectionately known as Mr. Cub. Ernie was truly a goodwill ambassador of baseball. By the way, he managed to hit more than five hundred home runs in an illustrious career.

Ernie seemed to always have a smile on his face. Most baseball players considered their sport to merely be a job, but not Ernie. He would come bounding into the clubhouse, grinning from ear to ear, and say, "Let's play two!" What he meant was that he was having so much fun playing one baseball game that two games would be double the fun. I doubt another modern-day player has ever uttered those words.

Ernie truly worked hard and cheerfully at baseball every day, just as though he was working for the Lord and not just for the Chicago Cubs. The way that he played baseball is role model behavior for any believer to emulate in his or her workplace. I doubt that many of us in the humdrum, eight-to-five, Monday through Friday workplace would come bounding into the office and shout, "Let's work from eight A.M.

until midnight today!" But when we are there, through our relationships and interactions, we have a chance to emulate Christ in all that we do and give our best effort. If you make an error, ask God and the person you hurt for forgiveness and get ready for the next play.

Prayer: Dear heavenly Father, when I think of Ernie Banks, my lasting impression is his smiling, enthusiastic face. May I be a vision of light today for someone I know. In the holy name of Jesus Christ, who died and rose just for me, amen.

BB26:
HOW DO YOUR STATS LOOK?

James 2:17, John 3:30

Faith without works is dead.

James 2:17

When I was six years old, I was obsessed with numbers and loved baseball. The numbers obsession was fed by the statistics on the baseball cards that I collected. Twenty-five cents would buy five cards and a stick of tasteless bubble gum. It was exciting to open the cards and hope that you got new cards. If you wound up with doubles, that was an opportunity for trading cards with your friends. I remember that first baseman Norm Cash of the Detroit Tigers hit .361 in 1962. I would entertain my family and friends with my memory of statistics on the cards.

Each spring, new baseball trading cards are produced. The previous year's stats for at-bats, runs, hits, and home runs are added as one row to the card and the player's total career numbers are updated.

Let's just suppose that there were trading cards for believers. What if your face was on a God's kingdom trading card that people could buy for 25 cents and a tasteless piece of bubble gum? What if your kingdom stats were updated for the previous year? The stats could include how many Sunday school lessons you taught, how many cards you sent to people, what percentage of your income you gave to the church, how many times you shared Christ with someone, and how many times you helped the poor. Would people see a positive change with your stats getting better each year, or would there be a general decline year after year? God expects us and needs us to get better as we go.

So take a few minutes and do a personal stat check. If you are lacking, be determined to be more obedient to God and ask him to change your heart anew.

Prayer: Most gracious God, may my stats reflect seeds that are sown that allow you to give the increase. Sometimes I sow and sometimes I water, but it is always you, our Lord God Almighty, who gives the increase. In Jesus's name, amen.

BB27:
OPENING DAY

Lamentations 3:22–23, John 8:32

His mercies are new every morning…

Lamentations 3:23

On opening day, baseball parks are filled across America as the major league season begins. Springtime is finally here, the green grass in the outfield is beautiful, the sunshine is warm after a harsh winter, and it just feels great to be at the ball park. The semicircles of red, white, and blue bunting are placed throughout the ball park to let you know that this day is different than the others. The bunting is a sign of the new hope that springs eternal in the hearts of the fans, many of whom believe that this will finally be the year that their team takes it all. Every team starts the season undefeated, but reality quickly sets in as some teams slide down the standings during the first month of the season.

As believers, we have the optimism and freedom of experiencing opening day each day of our lives. We can experience the joy because the truth, Jesus Christ, sets us free through the atoning blood of Christ and forgiveness from God. No matter what troubles face us on any given day, we can place our heads on the pillow at night and know that when we wake up tomorrow, we can feel the joy of opening day the following morning.

Prayer: Most holy Father God, I so appreciate your mercies and blessings that are new each day. May I realize the freshness of your unconditional love when I wake up each morning. I give you the thanks for my wonderful gifts. In Jesus's name, amen.

GOLF

GOLF01:
GIVE HIM THE GLORY IN
ALL THAT YOU DO

Philippians 4:13, Colossians 3:17

Whatever you do, in word or deed, do everything in the name of the Lord Jesus.

Colossians 3:17

I've always taken pride in my ability as an athlete, having earned ten varsity letters in high school although I graduated when I was only sixteen. I played college golf and still consider myself to be an athlete on the other side of the half century mark. But in all of my athletic competitions, I had never given God the glory during a contest until the Senior Club Championship golf tournament at Alpharetta CC in 2006. It wasn't the most competitive tournament, but there were some former college players. The tourney favorites were my good friends, Ralph, a former University of Alabama player who won the overall club championship by eight shots the previous weekend, and Jeff, a former college player from upstate New York and a big left hander, about six feet four inches, who hits it about nine miles.

I never really understood that when I played golf or took part in any activity, I should do it for God's glory. That approach seemed a little farfetched to me. Since I became a Christian in 2003, I certainly have tried to conduct myself with dignity, particularly after my pre-Jesus cursing and club-throwing antics. It just never occurred to me that I should stay connected to God during a four-hour round of golf.

During the front nine, I was conscious of God's presence, and I prayed breath prayers to stay calm and take whatever happened in stride. I eagled a par four and took a two-shot lead over Ralph to the back nine. Several times on the back nine, waiting to hit my next shot, I prayed, *God, please allow me to take one shot at a time and stay calm. I praise you for the peace that passes all understanding. I sure could use some of that peace right now!* I didn't pray to win, but I asked God to calm me so that I could perform my next shot well under the growing pressure of hanging onto the lead.

Ralph hung close, and Jeff got back in the tournament with four consecutive birdies. While I felt the pressure from my lead shrinking, I stayed focused and tried not to allow their performances to affect mine. I prayed silently, *God, I will glorify you if I win, and I will glorify you if I lose.* That was a prayer that I heard from Coach Taylor the previous afternoon, when Becca and I saw *Facing the Giants*. The glory that I wanted to give God was not where I finished but how I played. He gave me an inner peace that allowed me to perform well. The defining moment came on the par three seventeenth hole when I put my tee shot six inches from the cup. I tapped it in and won my first stroke-play tournament in twenty-five years. While I was very happy and pleased, I gave the glory to God. I felt that if I had not prayed and spoken to him during the round, I would not have been victorious.

Prayer: Father God, help me realize that you want to be part of every aspect of my life, no matter how insignificant I feel it is. Thank you for caring deeply about everything I do. When I do well, may you always receive the glory. In Jesus's name, amen.

GOLF02:
THE GOSPEL OF THE HOLE IN ONE

Matthew 7:13, 25:32; John 14:6

Heaven can only be entered by the narrow gate!

Matthew 7:13

The biggest thrill for any recreational golfer is to make a hole in one. Many golfers will play golf for a lifetime and never make one. *Golf Digest* once placed the odds of a hole in one at 33,000 to 1. When you consider the factors of the wind, yardage, ball flight, type of ball, hole location, contours of the green, type of club, and the speed of the green, it seems impossible. The hole is only four and a half inches wide, and your tee shot's margin of error is fifty yards in any direction.

Of course, the score for a hole in one is what? One. A one. Let it sink in. I find it interesting that the number 1 is the narrowest number of all the infinite combinations of numbers and integers. In golf, there is 2, 3, 4, 5, 6, the hockey stick 7, and the snowman 8. And there is little, skinny, narrow 1. Incredibly hard to achieve a 1 in golf. The Bible teaches us about the broad road and the narrow road. Matthew tells us that heaven can only be entered through the narrow gate. Isn't it interesting that from a distance, a narrow gate with high walls on either side is shaped like the number 1.

In life, it's humanly impossible to say no every time to the distractions of the broad road, with its broad gate and all of its sinful trappings. If sin weren't fun, no one would do it, I once heard. We're really comfortable going through the broad gate. Plenty of friends and colleagues are there with us at the broad gate as we bypass the narrow gate. But only the narrow gate leads to the immeasurable joy that can be ours instead of remaining disillusioned and unfulfilled by the temporary interludes of success and happiness of the broad road that can never satisfy us in the end.

Jesus didn't say he is "a" way. He is the Way, one Way. When you hear that somebody made a 1 or if you make a 1, stop and give thanks to the One who took your place on the cross. I'm thankful that I remembered to say, "Thank you, Jesus!" when I made my first hole in one. In June 2008, after thousands of rounds of golf over a forty-plus-year period, I holed an 8-iron from 165 yards on the eleventh hole at the East Course at Alpharetta Athletic Club.

Prayer: Dear heavenly Father, I am so thankful that you sent the One down from heaven to live among us and save us. And that the One is the one way to heaven. Thank you for Jesus, the One who died for me. In Jesus's name, amen.

GOLF03:
THE TRUTH SETS YOU FREE

John 8:32, 1 John 1:9

Then you will know the Truth, and the Truth will set you free.

John 8:32

My daughter Allison played the Atlanta Junior Golf Association (AJGA) summer circuit between her sophomore and junior high school years to gain tournament experience. Golf is a tough enough sport to learn without the added pressure of competing in tournaments, so she needed experience. Her first few events were difficult adjustments. We were usually up at five and on the road by six to travel to a course in North Georgia. Each time, there was a course that she had never seen, and several girls were quite good, which discouraged her at times. But Allison was very determined to improve.

But in one of her last events, her game came together. She was playing very consistently, and I was enjoying her good play as I walked with the other parents. On the sixth hole, Allison drove her ball into tall, wiry grass, but she played a beautiful escape to the fairway and salvaged her bogey. On the next tee, she drove it long and straight down the fairway, and I saw a smile crease her face in the morning sunlight. Allison chatted with Chelsea, her fellow competitor, as she walked toward her ball for her second shot. As she looked at the ball, I saw her do what I would describe as a double take. She walked toward us, and I could see tears forming in her eyes. Allison walked to the AJGA volunteer with her group and said, "That's not my ball. I must have played the wrong ball out of the rough." I was just heartbroken for her because she was finally playing well in a tournament. Allison was disqualified for playing the wrong ball. The volunteer said, "Allison, it took a lot of courage to come over and tell me." Chelsea tried to console her, and Chelsea's mother said, "Allison, you can watch my money any time!" It was a beautiful compliment and helped ease the sting.

As badly as the DQ hurt, Allison has been able to recall that situation and remember how she acted with integrity. She created a life lesson that carried into her college and professional work careers. She told the truth, and she remains free from wondering if she had made a different choice to keep playing. By the way, the tournament experience paid off, as Allison was one of three players to play for her team at region and state the following year. Her Lassiter HS team won the state championship. Allison told her granddad, who won a state title in basketball exactly fifty years before, "We've got another state champ in the family!"

Jesus taught his disciples, "Then you will know the truth, and the truth will set you free." When we fail to follow through with integrity and complete honesty, it will haunt us, but as believers we are not condemned (Romans 8:1). If we confess our sins, God is faithful and just and will forgive our sins and cleanse us from all unrighteousness. Once you've confessed, accept God's forgiveness and move forward to the next round. Don't be looking four or five holes back. Forgive and forget is what God does, and so should you. Learn from your experience and move on with your life.

Prayer: Father God, it's so cool the way you give us life lessons to teach us how to behave. Thank you for the presence of the Holy Spirit in our lives that prompts us when the clerk gives us too much money back, when our ball moves in the fairway, when the entire story needs to be told, and when we make decisions with integrity. Forgive me when I fail you, and help me accept your forgiveness and cleanse me anew. In Jesus's name, amen.

GOLF04: TAKE CHRIST INTO YOUR WORKPLACE

Proverbs 27:17

Iron sharpens iron, so a man sharpens the countenance of his friend.

I shared this story with the golfers at the Mark Richt FCA tournament in Athens in May 2007. This picture was taken by Chad, the son of my very good friend, Ralph, at the Monday Masters practice round. The two golfers are Zach Johnson (L), who would become the 2007 champion just six days later, and Larry Mize (R), the 1987 Masters champion. The significance of this seemingly random photograph is that two Christians are speaking. Larry is probably sharing course knowledge and strategy with Zach, but perhaps they also shared the Word and some faith stories. Zach has no idea that he would become the Masters champ.

After he finished his Sunday round, Zach told the CBS announcer and a national TV audience that he felt that Jesus was with him during the back nine on Sunday. Zach said that he was able to remain calm and that the victory was even more special because it occurred on Easter Sunday. The moral of the story: Zach invited Jesus to become part of his work day. Zach turned to Jesus to bring him peace during a very tense and important time in the midst of his workday. At the end, instead of taking the credit, Zach gave God all the glory. Isn't Zach's example a great golf lesson for us to take Christ into the place where we are working, whether it is at the office or at school? When we have a tough assignment or tough test, Jesus is always there for us.

Prayer: Father God, thank you for always being there for me no matter where I am or what I am doing. Help me shine my light in all situations so I can bring you glory. In Jesus's precious name, amen.

Zach Johnson (L) and Larry Mize (R) on the putting green
before the Masters practice round

GOLF05:
SET YOUR FACE LIKE FLINT

Isaiah 50:7

Because the Lord God helps me, I will not be dismayed. Therefore I will set my face like flint to do His will, and I know that I will triumph.

One Monday morning, a friend had just given me two badges to the Masters for the final round that concluded on Monday due to rain delays. After our nine o'clock class, Joel and I drove to our friend's apartment and literally dragged him out of bed to go to Augusta for the final round.

We arrived in Augusta and hurried breathlessly to the course just in time to see Jack Nicklaus begin his final day charge. Jack was eight shots back and needed a final round 64 to get in the hunt after a 77 the previous day. He birdied the first and second holes, and a huge crowd, hoping for some final round magic, followed Jack.

He parred the third and then inexplicably three-putted the par-3 fourth for a momentum-killing bogey. That would make the task really difficult now. I made my way to the ropes directly behind the fifth tee box as Jack and his caddie, Angelo Argea, walked over. Nicklaus, with his blond mane and unbelievable talent and strong work ethic, was on his way to becoming the greatest player in the history of the game.

Jack rarely showed strong emotion, but he was clearly perturbed by the three-putt. He rested his left arm on Angelo's shoulder and cleaned the grass out of his cleats using his divot repair tool.

Actually, he did more than clean the grass out. He ripped the grass out because he was still smoldering from the lost momentum. The fifth hole is a long, uphill par 4. Jack took a very aggressive line over the bunkers, set his jaw firmly with determination, and just smoked a BB over the bunker, setting up a short iron to the green, followed by two more birdies for a 32. He birdied the eighteenth hole to close with a 66, which would leave him two shots back.

Recalling how Jack set his jaw and dug down for something extra after the disappointing three-putt made me think about this verse from Isaiah. Sometimes, the Lord will give us a task to do, and we encounter dissension, or a lack of support, or roadblocks seemingly materialize out of nowhere. As believers, let's recall that we can set our jaw firmly and tap his great power through the Holy Spirit who lives within us. With God's power within us, we can overcome those obstacles and be victorious for his kingdom.

Prayer: Father, you never promised us that this life would be easy. When tough times come, may I know that your power is within me to face the difficulties and overcome them. Thank you, Lord. In Jesus's name, amen.

GOLF06:
TURNING TRAGEDY
INTO TRIUMPH

Matthew 28:1–9, John 3:16–17

He is not here, he has risen, as he has said …

Matthew 28:6

Ben Hogan was one of the greatest golfers in history. Known as the Ice Man for his steely concentration and quiet demeanor, Hogan overcame a great personal setback to play the best golf of his career three years after a near-fatal accident. In 1950, Hogan and his wife, Valerie, were hit head on by a bus on a dark, foggy road in Texas. Ben almost died, and his doctors considered tying off his legs, which would have left them useless. Though he made a miraculous recovery and was able to walk again, the doctors still said that he would never play competitive golf. But through tremendous perseverance and hard work, Hogan not only recovered but won the only three major championships that he entered in 1953. Tragedy was overcome by triumph to the delight of the sports world and his legion of fans.

Jesus showed all of us how tragedy was overcome by triumph. When he took a savage beating and was nailed to the cross, all hope appeared lost for his disciples and followers, who scattered after learning of his demise. His enemies jeered Jesus and cried, "Save yourself! Come down if you are the Son of God!" But Jesus triumphed over tragedy three days later when he rose from the grave and met two of his apostles on the road to Emmaus. He defeated death forever.

You can also overcome tragedy and live a triumphant life. God created a plan for your life to know him and experience joy as a believer, a person who has committed his life to Jesus Christ. Perhaps you have lost hope or seemingly lost your way. You can find your way to Christ through repentance and ask him to come into your life. Repentance, which is turning from sin and turning toward God, is absolutely necessary. Because without repentance, no matter how hard you try, your life will end in tragedy because you will be separated from God forever. When you die a physical death, you will also die spiritually if you don't know Christ. Turn tragedy into triumph and live eternally through trust and faith in Jesus Christ, the Living Son of God, and the One who took my place on the cross.

Prayer: Most holy God, giver of all good things, including the grace that I cannot earn, help me turn tragedy into triumph for eternity through your Son, Jesus Christ, who came into the world not to condemn me but to save me. In Jesus's name, amen.

GOLF07: A TRIBUTE TO CORA, JACK'S BIGGEST FAN

Psalm 119:105, Jeremiah 6:16

Thy Word is a lamp unto my feet, and a light unto my path.

Psalm 119:105

I remember the first time that I saw my dear friend, Cora. I was at my first Masters in 1973 when I was seventeen when I found out what a thrill it was to watch Jack Nicklaus, the Golden Bear, play golf for eighteen holes at Augusta. I decided to follow Jack on Saturday, but I didn't know the best way to get around the course. As Jack approached the green on the third hole to enthusiastic applause, I heard a high-pitched woman's voice. "Go get 'em, Jack!" Jack waved his hand in acknowledgment, and that's when I saw Cora. She was about five feet tall and was wearing a gold Jack's Pack pendant in the shape of a bear. Her beautiful silver hair was in a bun, and she wore sunglasses and a visor to shield her face from the sun. She also seemed to know everybody around her.

As I walked the course, I found out it was tough to get close to Jack. On some holes, I would fall behind no matter how fast I walked to keep up. I would miss the timing for the crosswalk and be forced to wait for the group behind Jack to come through. Then I would hurry (without running, of course) to the next hole.

I kept noticing how this charming little woman was always in the right place. She didn't seem to be out of breath and chatted away until the next shot. So I got smart. *I will follow her, and then I'll be in the right place.* On the back nine, I introduced myself to Cora because I was a huge Jack fan, and she sort of adopted me from that point forward.

Cora walked almost every round with Jack for almost forty years beginning in 1963. She would pick his group up on number one fairway and follow him through his final putt on eighteen. Cora would record his putts for each hole on her program, and she never sat in the bleachers. After Jack completed his round, she walked home to nearby Cherry Lane. In 1986, I remember standing with her on seventeen when Seve Ballesteros hit his second shot in the water on fifteen, opening the door for Jack to win with a back nine thirty for his sixth green jacket. On seventeen came the putt when Jack lifts his putter in the air and Verne Lundquist screams, "Yes, sir!" I never saw anybody else at the Masters support Jack as loyally as Cora. She was indeed Jack's biggest fan at Augusta.

That sun-kissed Saturday afternoon at Augusta National began a wonderful friendship of about thirty-five years. After Cora could no longer walk the course, our family would still park in her yard on Cherry Lane and visit with her husband, affectionately known as "her Jack," and their daughter, Christy. When Cora passed away, Jack and Christy received a wonderful note from Barbara and Jack Nicklaus.

Cora had a specific path that she followed round after round (see Jeremiah 6:16) that put her in the best place to see the action. I wasted a lot of steps and energy trying to see the same action because of my lack of knowledge and experience. Psalm 119:105 says that the Word is a Lamp unto our feet and a Light unto our path. When we don't follow the teachings of the Word, we cost ourselves a lot of steps and energy. But if we learn the Scriptures and follow the guidance provided there by God, we will be in the right place much more often. We will waste less energy in addressing the consequences that inevitably occur when we make bad decisions. Let's study his Word so that we will know the path of righteousness. When we stay on the right path, God blesses us with untold riches.

Prayer: Father God, thank you for the wonderful people we meet and the eternal relationships that we develop through sports. May I realize that sports are a wonderful gift that can be used to help people experience your mighty love. In the holy name of Jesus Christ, amen.

Footnote: Cora never wanted anyone to tie Jack's record of six Masters victories. When Tiger Woods came close to winning his fifth Masters one year, I found out why he lost when I got back to Cora's house. When Tiger would putt, Cora would put her thumb over the hole on TV so that the ball wouldn't go in.

GOLF08:
DOES GOD HAVE A TIGER BY THE TAIL?

1 Samuel 12:1–12; Psalm 41:4, 51:4

Against you alone, Lord, have I sinned...

Psalm 51:4

Tiger Woods was riding high at the top of his profession in the fall of 2009. Then came the stunning news that Tiger Woods was reported to be in serious condition in an Orlando hospital after an early morning car accident. This incorrect story was soon followed by a growing list of disturbing allegations of his unfaithfulness. Tiger's fall soon became a top news story around the world and the butt of countless jokes.

Tiger's idyllic life unraveled before his eyes. It would be really easy to give up on Tiger and throw him under the bus, but remember that God never gives up on us no matter how many times we mess up. When God looks at our personal sin, he doesn't weigh it or measure it. In God's eyes, sin is sin, period, and sin separates a person from God. He doesn't rank order it or compare it to the sins of other people, as many are doing as they push Tiger below their names in the pecking order of worst sinners.

Despite his fame and fortune, Tiger is no different than you and me. You, Tiger, and I are all one on one with God. Any sins are between the individual and God. A believer should be in prayer for any person that has fallen. Before a person throws the next stone at someone, perhaps it's a good time to take stock to see if there is a speck in the left eye or a log in the right eye. Jesus taught us that lust is the same as adultery, and hatred is the same as murder.

King David was also riding high. He was a man after God's own heart and was highly favored by God. David had conquered many tribes in recent battles. Perhaps he was complacent and bored on the day that he saw the stunning Bathsheba bathing on a rooftop. He had to have her, so he sent her husband, Uriah, into a dangerous battle and more or less instructed his army, "Okay. When the battle begins, on the count of three, everybody but Uriah take two big steps backward. Got it?" Uriah was killed, which paved the way for David to bring Bathsheba into the palace.

That's when God sent a man named Nathan to give David a little coaching. Nathan told David the story of a rich man who killed a poor man's only lamb, which crushed the poor man. David was appalled and called for the rich man to be put to death, but first, the rich man should repay the poor man with four ewes, David said. Nathan looked David in the eye and said, "You are the man."

Imagine the shivers that went through David's body and the sinking feeling in his stomach the instant that he realized how he had sinned against God. He cried out, "Against you alone, Lord, have I sinned." Nathan assured him that God would honor his confession and forgive his sins. David had lied to Uriah, coveted and stolen another man's wife, dishonored his family with his actions, and put his selfish desires above God and all that he knew to be honorable and virtuous. If the Ten Commandments represent ten bowling pins, David had just rolled a strike.

Will God grind Tiger to powder until he looks upward, thanks God for his mercy, and accepts God's free gift of grace available to all? I invite you to join me in praying that Tiger will repent and receive Christ. Consider the possibilities for God's kingdom. Many would be drawn to the Savior through evidence of fruit borne if Tiger's heart were changed by Christ. But first, Tiger must look heavenward and cry, as David did, "Against you alone, Lord, have I sinned."

Prayer: Dear Father God, help me learn from my mistakes and the mistakes of others so that I don't repeat them. I pray for salvation for Tiger and for those who don't know you as Savior. Help me let you do the judging, and I will do the praying. In Jesus's name, amen.

GOLF09:
BERNHARD LANGER

Romans 6:23

For the wages of sin is death, but the gift of God is eternal life through Jesus Christ.

Bernhard Langer began his golf career in Germany as a teenage apprentice and soon inherited the putting yips, which is an involuntary reflex that can send the ball speeding by the hole and off the green! He overcame that dilemma and later won golf's most prestigious event, the Masters Tournament, in 1985 and 1995. The soft-spoken German, who now resides in the United States, has achieved an illustrious career on the Champions Tour for golfers fifty and over. He shared this story of how he came to know Christ as his Savior.

"The week after I won the 1985 Masters, I was invited by a friend and fellow touring pro to come to the PGA Tour Bible Study.

"Something was missing. My priorities were golf, golf, more golf, then myself, and finally a little time with my wife. Every now and then, I prayed. I went to church. But if my golf game was not good, my whole life was miserable and I made everyone around me miserable.

"That night was the first time in my life that I heard that I needed to be 'reborn.' I was amazed to realize that the only way to have eternal life is through Jesus Christ—which he died for our sins. After understanding that God loved me so much that he sent his only Son to die for my sins, it was natural for me to ask the Lord into my life…I've seen tremendous changes in my life, my marriage, and my whole outlook. My priorities have changed. They're now where they should be: God first, family second, and then my career."

Prayer: Dear Jesus, thank you for this story of how we must be reborn to enter the kingdom of God. In fact, it's the same message that you shared with Nicodemus almost 2,000 years ago. May I share with others that only through spiritual rebirth is it possible to enter the gates of heaven. In Jesus's name, amen.

GOLF10:
LARRY MIZE

John 15:5

I am the Vine, you are the branches. He who abides in Me, and I in him, bears much fruit; apart from Me you can do nothing.

Larry Mize has enjoyed a successful career as a PGA Tour professional and as a member of the Champions Tour. A native of Augusta, Georgia, Larry dreamed as a young man of being good enough to play in the Masters. Not only did he achieve his first goal, but incredibly he won the major championship that he cherished more than any other. On the second playoff hole of the 1987 Masters, Larry's one-hundred-foot chip on the par 4 eleventh hole landed on the green, checked, and rolled into the hole. He leaped to celebrate one of golf history's biggest shots.

After that incredible win, a setback in his career occurred that he could not have seen coming. Two years later, Larry wanted to quit golf because he was playing so poorly. He was thinking of himself as Larry Mize, Masters Champion, rather than as a person who is capable of making mistakes. Then Larry Moody, a Bible study leader on the PGA Tour, counseled him.

"Your significance doesn't come from being a professional golfer or a Masters champion ... from what you've accomplished or what you do. It comes from knowing you're a child of God…that makes you significant no matter what the world says."

If only your job or performance makes you significant, then your life will be like a roller coaster. You have infinite worth because God sent his only Son, Jesus Christ, to die for us.

Prayer: Father God, it seems that either I'm grinding because things aren't going well, or when they do, it is easy for me to get a swelled head. Help me stay grounded in the fact that becoming a Christian will always be the greatest thing that I have going for me. In Jesus's holy name, amen.

GOLF11:
ZACH JOHNSON

Isaiah 53:5

By his wounds, we are healed.

Zach Johnson is a native of Iowa who has enjoyed a great deal of success on the PGA Tour. He has won seven PGA Tour titles and was a Ryder Cup team member in 2006 and 2010.

Zach's two-shot victory over Tiger Woods at the 2007 Masters Tournament on Easter Sunday surprised those inside and outside the golf world but came as no surprise to those who know him. Johnson used the occasion to boldly proclaim his love and faith in Jesus Christ. He became the second professing Christian to win the Masters Tournament on Easter Sunday.

Johnson credited his faith in God and the counsel of longtime PGA Tour chaplain Larry Moody of Search Ministry, whose Bible study Johnson attends on a weekly basis, for allowing him to remain calm, cool, and collected in the competitive and often chaotic final round.

"Because it's Easter today, I want to say, 'Thank you, Jesus,'" Johnson said at the ceremony on the practice green. "Being Easter Sunday, I feel very blessed and honored and I feel like there was a power that was walking with me and guiding me. So that's where things stand. You know, I feel very blessed and honored to be here."

Zach beating Tiger down the stretch was sort of like David beating Goliath. When Zach faced his biggest moments on the back nine, he remembered that God was with him to give him strength and courage. When David slew Goliath, he was also conscious that God was by his side. Both of them gave God the glory.

Prayer: Father God, thank you for an athlete who thought about you during the most important tournament of his life. When I am under stress, and there is a lot on the line, may I remember to include you and your power to keep me calm under pressure so that I can perform to the best of my ability. In Jesus's name, amen.

GOLF12:
PAYNE STEWART (1965–1999)

2 Timothy 4:7

I have fought the good fight. I have finished the race. I have kept the faith.

Payne Stewart was one of the most colorful golfers of his era. He was known for his stylish knickers that he wore to set himself apart from the other golfers. Payne was also quite a practical joker. When Paul Azinger holed a bunker shot on the seventy-second hole to beat him by one at the 1993 Memorial Tournament, Payne was among the first people to congratulate his close friend. After the press conference Paul went back to the locker room to change into his street shoes, which were now full of mashed bananas, thanks to Payne!

Payne had come to a personal relationship with Jesus Christ not long before his life on earth came to a stunning end. It was a tragedy that sent shockwaves around the world. On October 25, 1999, a small plane plummeted to the ground near Mina, South Dakota, killing everyone aboard. Among them was golfing great Payne Stewart.

Just a few months earlier, he had captured the US Open in storybook fashion after a devastating loss in the same tournament the year before. Payne was best known among his peers for his flamboyant knickers, rhythmic golf swing, and the pranks that he pulled as a practical joker. But Payne had made huge strides in his faith earlier that year. When he accepted the trophy, he surprised many people by saying, "First of all, I have to give thanks to the Lord. If it weren't for the faith that I have in him, I wouldn't have been able to have the faith that I had in myself on the golf course…I'm proud of the fact that my faith in God is so much stronger, and I'm so much more at peace with myself than I've ever been in my life."

Often we are led to believe that improved performance on the athletic field comes strictly from working harder and practicing more. But Payne Stewart showed us that the key to winning the Open was his growth in Christ that helped him keep his wits about him in golf's most pressure-packed event.

When Payne won the US Open on Father's Day, he obviously had no idea that he would leave this life behind less than six months later. The good news is that his wife and two children found some comfort because they knew Payne's final destination was the fairways of heaven. At Payne's memorial service, in recognition of his distinctive knickers, Paul Azinger paused at the podium and stuffed his pants legs into his socks in a tribute to his brother in Christ.

Prayer: Father God, thank you for the legacy of Payne Stewart, a man remembered not only for the joy with which he played the game of golf, but for the joy that he received from finishing his race with Christ as his Lord. In Jesus's name, amen.

GOLF13:
LARRY NELSON

Romans 5:8

But God demonstrates His own love toward us, in that while we were still sinners, Christ died for us.

Larry Nelson is a three-time major championship winner and a member of the World Golf Hall of Fame. His legacy in golf is the quiet grace and humility that he has displayed while winning golf's most prestigious titles. Larry was named the winner of the 2011 PGA Distinguished Service award for his work with local charities.

Larry's career began unlike few others. After returning from a tour in Vietnam, he played golf for the first time at the age of 21. He broke 70 in less than a year and earned his PGA Tour card in 1974. Larry shared the story of how he came to know Jesus Christ one year later.

The quiet Georgian was recuperating from an automobile accident in San Diego in 1975, and with a hotel Bible in his hand, began to read. He recalled, "I had heard Billy Graham speak in Charlotte the year before and remembered that he said, 'If you have any questions about your relationship with the Lord, read the gospel of John and the book of Romans.'"

Nelson began to read in Romans and discovered that "all have sinned and come short of the glory of God." He realized that even though he had gone to church since he was a small child, he was not good enough to inherit eternal life on his own merits. After reading in Romans that Christ died for us while we were still sinners, Nelson asked Jesus to come into his life and experienced God's saving grace.

Larry's successful golf career shows us that it's never too late to find one's true talents in life. He used his skills effectively to put himself in a position to win two of golf's greatest championships. When he found himself with plenty of time on his hands in San Diego, he put himself in a position to receive eternal grace, God's greatest gift.

Prayer: Father God, thank you for the legacy of Larry Nelson and that not only will golf fans remember the majors that he won, but they will especially remember the demeanor of this champion who reflected the qualities of Christ regardless of whether he won or lost. In the holy name of Jesus Christ, amen.

GOLF14:
PAUL AZINGER

John 11:25–26

Jesus said to her, "I am the resurrection and the life. Whoever believes in me, though he die, yet shall he live. And everyone who lives and believes in me shall never die. Do you believe this?"

In 1993, Paul Azinger won the PGA Championship. He was at the height of his career, one of the top money winners on the tour. Then it happened. At age thirty-three, he was diagnosed with cancer, non-Hodgkin's lymphoma.

"A genuine feeling of fear came over me," he says. "I realized I could die. Everything I had accomplished in golf became meaningless to me. Then I remembered something that Larry Moody, who teaches a Bible study on the PGA Tour, said to me.

"Larry said, 'Zinger, we're not in the land of the living heading toward the land of the dying. We're in the land of the dying heading toward the land of the living.'"

Even the fear of death will step aside for someone who has the resurrection life of Jesus living inside them.

After Paul's successful battle with cancer, he came back to compete on the PGA Tour, became an ABC golf analyst, and later became the captain of America's winning Ryder Cup team in 2008.

Paul learned to place his trust in God, who has the power to heal us from cancer and other diseases. We will never know this side of heaven why some people are healed and some are not. But God understands when we are afraid; he hears our prayers and answers them according to his divine will.

Prayer: Most gracious Healer, help me to remember that you are the Great Physician and Healer. Thank you for brothers in Christ such as Larry Moody, who give me godly advice when I need it most. When I encounter a problem, may I remember to come to you for comfort and strength. In Jesus's name, amen.

GOLF15:
STEWART CINK

John 3:16

For God so loved the world, that He gave his only begotten Son, that whosoever should believe in Him, will not perish but have everlasting life.

One of Stewart Cink's biggest claims to fame is that he was the number one spoiler of Tiger Woods's unprecedented amateur career. Stewart often beat Tiger or finished higher than Tiger in important collegiate tournaments. A graduate of Georgia Tech, Stewart has won thirteen professional tournaments worldwide, including the 2009 British Open Championship. He has been a member of four President's Cup teams and five Ryder Cup teams, including the victorious 2008 Ryder Cup team.

In 2004, Stewart Cink and his pastor from Duluth First Baptist Church traveled to Japan to do some mission work. Many Japanese have an intense interest in golf and are well-acquainted with top PGA celebrities. Consequently, the six-foot-four-inch tall Cink used not only his physical height but his stature as a golfer as the platform upon which to share his faith. Cink spoke to prominent business executives about golf and shared his testimony.

"Though it took me a few years, the most important lesson I ever learned was that the way to heaven leads directly through Jesus Christ and only through Him," Cink testifies. "My relationship with Christ is now the central part of my life. I am a better father to my two boys. I am a better husband to my wife, and I am a better golfer now that the Lord is walking with me in the fairways and through the rough."

Prayer: Father God, help me realize as Stewart did that the closer that I am in knowing Christ, the better person I will become in all of my personal relationships. Thank you for the most important relationship of all, which is the eternal one with Jesus. In Jesus's name, amen.

GOLF16:
TOM LEHMAN

2 Corinthians 5:17

When someone becomes a Christian, he becomes a new person inside. He is not the same anymore. A new life has begun!

After playing college golf at the University of Minnesota, Tom Lehman survived the rigors of playing second-tier golf tours in the United States and even the Asian Tour before finally earning his card on the PGA Tour.

His biggest tournament win came at the prestigious 1996 British Open Championship with his father in attendance. But his win led to an assurance that no worldly victory, no matter how exciting, can ever approach the ultimate victory of knowing Jesus Christ. Here is how Tom recalls the experience.

"I'll never forget the day I won the British Open, all the awards ceremonies, the champagne toast with the R & A, the endless interviews. What a feeling of exhilaration!

"Winning the British Open was a thrill of a lifetime. But I learned a long time ago that the thrill of victory is fleeting. It's not long before you find yourself asking, 'What's next?'

"As much as I longed to win a major championship, it didn't change anything. I was still the same person as before. I had the same hang-ups, the same problems, and even some new ones.

"The Bible says, 'All men are like grass and their glory is like the flowers of the field. The grass withers and the flowers fall.'

"So what is it that lasts? The only thing that has given my life true meaning: my relationship with Jesus Christ."

Lehman learned that even winning one of the ultimate championships in golf pales in comparison to knowing Christ as your Savior and Lord and to have the peace and assurance that God is with you each day of your life.

Prayer: Dear Father, thank you for the lesson to be learned of staying grounded in Christ no matter how thrilling our victories are in this world. I thank you for the ultimate victory of knowing Christ and being in heaven with him one day. In the holy name of Jesus, amen.

GOLF17: KENNY PERRY

Romans 12:12

Be glad for all that God is planning for you. Be patient in trouble and prayerful always.

When Kenny Perry attempted to qualify for the PGA Tour, he agreed to a unique sponsorship. A man gave him $5,000 for qualifying school. If he failed to qualify, he didn't have to pay it back. If he qualified, he agreed to give 5 percent of his earnings to David Lipscomb University in Nashville, Tennessee. Kenny has honored this pledge throughout his career.

It looked like a storybook ending to cap a career that blossomed late. Kenny Perry experienced the thrill of a lifetime in his home state of Kentucky, when he played well as a member of the first victorious US Ryder Cup Team in a decade. He had four wins on the PGA Tour in the eighteen months leading up to the 2009 Masters. Kenny was one par away from being the oldest man to win the Masters after stuffing an 8-iron within six inches of the cup on the legendary sixteenth hole. But Kenny was unable to finish off his round, and he bogeyed the last two holes and eventually lost in a playoff.

However, Kenny allowed the Lord's Light to shine during the play-off, when he applauded Angel Cabrera's miracle par save from the trees, and again when he was incredibly gracious after perhaps the most disappointing hour of his golf career. Kenny said after his heartbreaking loss, "I have got my mom struggling with cancer, my dad's struggling [with his heart]. I have got a lot of people who are hurting right now and here I am playing golf for a living and having the time of my life. So I'm not going there. I'm not going to play 'pity on me.' And you know what? I'm going to enjoy it. I really am. I fought hard and I was proud of the way I hung in there."

Kenny demonstrated that God's grace can surface during a time of significant disappointment. He honored his parents and maintained his perspective that there is much more to life than winning a major golf tournament.

Prayer: Father God, in a day when so many athletes and coaches are less than gracious in defeat, thank you for the lessons of generosity, humility, and good sportsmanship from Kenny Perry. Help me keep my victories and defeats in proper perspective to my loved ones around me. In Jesus's name, amen.

GOLF18:
GARY PLAYER

Ephesians 5:20

Give thanks for everything to our God and Father in the name of our Lord Jesus Christ.

Gary Player is a nine-time major championship winner who has flown millions of miles around the world in his fifty plus years in professional golf. He has traveled more miles than any golfer and played in more Masters tournaments (51) than any player in history. Gary played his final round in the Masters on the Friday of the 2009 tournament. The fans applauded him at each green for being a three-time Masters champion and for the determination and humility that he consistently displayed.

This question came from a writer after his last Masters round: "Can you remember the reception you had on the eighteenth? Was that louder than when you won all your jackets?"

Gary replied, "No question. Ten times more. I'll never forget that as long as I live. It just went on and on and on from all sides."

He continued, "But it happened on every single hole. All thirty-six holes, I got a standing ovation. I wish I had words to …I wish, as I had just mentioned, the vocabulary of Winston Churchill to say the correct thing, but it was a feast. It was something you'll never, ever forget. You'll go to your grave knowing you had tremendous love showered upon yourself."

Gary said, "I'm saying it, and I'm repeating myself, that I said it at the dinner the other night. We can all say a prayer, and everybody has a choice of believing or not, but a man never stands so tall as when he's on his knees."

Player received tributes around the course that day. In front of the final green, he got on his knees and gave God the glory, the honor, and the praise.

Prayer: Father God, thank you for the legacy of Gary Player, a man small in stature but a giant among his peers for his accomplishments both on and off the golf course. May I be reminded that when I want to stand tall, I need to make it happen on my knees. In the precious name of Jesus, amen.

GOLF19:
PAT SUMMERALL

Jeremiah 29:13

You will seek me and find me when you seek me with your
whole heart.

Pat Summerall was a professional football player for the New York
Giants in the 1950s, but he is better known for his career as a broadcaster. Ironically he began his broadcasting career after fielding a phone
call for his teammate, Giants quarterback Charley Connerly. A TV station called to invite Connerly to try out for a broadcasting job, and Pat
talked the station into giving him an audition too!

Pat eventually became one of the all-time great sportscasters, and
he called thirty Masters tournaments for CBS Sports. He was well
known for being able to paint the big picture by saying more with
fewer words. Everything seemed to come easy for Pat since his rise as
a sportscaster.

But Pat glorified in himself and eventually became an alcoholic.
He was shocked into entering the Betty Ford clinic when his daughter
said she was ashamed to share his last name. After stubbornly entering
the clinic, Pat began to read the Bible and kept reading it after leaving
the clinic thirty-three days later. (The first five days didn't count; he
was so angry.)

He committed his life to Christ in 1992 and underwent a liver
transplant in 2004. After expressing guilt over someone else dying so

that he could live, his pastor replied, "Because God is not done with you yet!"

In his first visit to Augusta since his liver transplant, Pat triumphantly but humbly returned for Masters week 2009 and gave his testimony to over a thousand people at the prayer breakfast on Masters Tuesday.

Pat and all of us can be thankful that we serve a God who never gives up on us and will never stop pursuing us, no matter how far we have strayed from him.

Prayer: Father God, thank you for your pursuit of me that never ends. You never give up on me regardless of how badly I have messed up. Thank you for your eternal promise of a life in Christ if only I will hold up my end of the deal. In Jesus's name, amen.

GOLF20:
UP AND DOWN

Lamentations 3:22–23

His mercies are new every morning...

Lamentations 3:23

One key to making a good score in golf is to be a good chipper and putter. Even the best players miss the green with their approach shots a third of the time, or six out of eighteen holes. There is nothing like a great pitch and a well-holed eight-footer to give you momentum and keep your round going. Getting it up on the green and down in one putt is called an up and down.

When I played on my college golf team, my roommate, Tim Fulcher, was our number-one player, not because he hit the ball further than anyone but because he could chip and putt with the best of them. During my sophomore season, we played in a regional championship at Stone Mountain and one of his competitors was muttering to himself as he approached the eighteenth green. When someone asked him what the matter was, he whined, "That guy (Tim) could get it up and down out of a trash can!" Fulcher had gotten it up and down seven times on the back nine on his way to winning individual medalist honors.

Another player who was pretty doggone good at getting it up and down was Tom Watson. Jack Nicklaus was gunning for a record fifth US Open Championship, and he and Watson were tied. Watson hooked his approach shot to the left of the green into tall rough, but he drew a favorable lie. When his caddie, Bruce Edwards, encouraged him to chip it close, Watson said, "Close? I'm gonna make it." He did and ran a victory lap around the green, pointing at Bruce Edwards in an "I told you so!" gesture of happiness and exultation.

Just as an up and down is important for golfers to maintain good scores, an up and down is important for believers to maintain good standing with God. Too often, when we are up, when things are going exceedingly well, we forget to get down on our knees and thank God for the abundant blessings that he gives us each day. We need to remember that each day he gives us is a blessing in itself, and our mercies are new every morning. When we are down because of circumstances, we can be lifted up by the joy that comes from knowing that Christ understands and has been through whatever we're going through. Jesus also intercedes on our behalf, and the Holy Spirit supplies a deeper understanding of what we are really trying to tell God when the right words just won't come out.

So remember, the simple key to an up and down for a believer is being on our knees when we are up and being on our knees when we are down. That's how you build a lasting relationship with the Father.

Prayer: Dear Father, when I need to be lifted up, help me get down on my knees. Only your love, mercy, and grace can lift me up. I thank you for your saving grace from which I can draw joy each day. In the holy name of the Risen One, amen.

GOLF21:
WHAT REALLY MATTERS

2 Corinthians 5:17

When someone becomes a Christian, he becomes a new person inside. He is not the same anymore, a new life has begun.

I was watching the AT&T Pebble Beach National Pro-Am on TV, and a tribute to the late Danny Gans appeared on the screen. Sadly, Danny Gans had passed away since the last Pro-Am, and the final credit read "Danny Gans (1956–2009)." I reflected that Danny and I probably shared several similarities: first of all, a love for golf and a love for Pebble Beach, one of the world's most breathtaking golf courses. He and I shared the same first name: Danny. We were both fathers. We both had four letters in our last names. He and I were virtually the same age when he passed. I was born in 1955, and he was born in 1956. One similarity that we did not share is that he apparently made millions of dollars per year as an impersonator in the Las Vegas casinos.

One of the most glorious meetings of land and sea is how Pebble Beach has long been described. I had the good fortune of attending the AT&T Pebble Beach Pro-Am tournament in 2000 and 2001 and playing several area courses. What a thrill it was to be part of the spectacle as a spectator. It's a sun-kissed Saturday, the surf is crashing along the par five eighteenth, it's seventy-two degrees when there is snow in the east, and the stars of golf and entertainment are on display. The entertainers joke with the crowds, sign autographs, and occasionally hit a decent shot or make a putt. The tournament ends at 3:00 P.M. in the West since TV needs a 6:00 P.M. finish in the East. One of the coolest golf moments that I ever had was sitting on the seventh tee after tournament play had concluded. I was facing Carmel Bay and listening to stories about the tournament from one of the groundskeepers. For a golf fan, it doesn't get much better.

I was almost three years from being saved the last time I went to the AT&T Pebble Beach Pro-Am. At the time, I lived for moments like Pebble Beach to fill the God-shaped vacuum in my heart. When I experienced a great sports thrill, I wanted another one. But after I was saved, moments like that didn't hold the same attraction. I am grateful that I experienced Pebble and Augusta National, but if I never went back, it would be okay. Events like that just don't grab me like they once did. It has everything to do with my attitude in Christ once I received him. It's his eternal moments that I attempt to live for.

I never knew Danny Gans, but I hoped that at that moment, there was life in eternity for him with God, beyond the ice plants and crashing waves of Pebble Beach, a very special place.

Prayer: Father God, it's cool when I get to do neat stuff and call my friends and brag to them about where I am. But help me keep the right perspective and include you there with me to enjoy the moment. I praise you for the special opportunities that I have through sports and hope that I honor you during those good times. In Jesus's name, amen.

GOLF22:
HEAVEN'S GRAND SLAM (GOLF)

Jeremiah 29:11, Romans 5:8, 1 John 1:9,
John 3:16, Ephesians 2:8

But by grace you have been saved through faith …

Ephesians 2:8

Each year, the best golfers in the world attempt to achieve immortality in golf's history book by winning one of the four major championships. It's only happened once that a golfer won all four majors in the same year. That feat was achieved by the incomparable sportsman and gentleman, Bobby Jones from Atlanta, Georgia, in 1930. His dear friend, the writer O. B. Keeler, chronicled Bobby's greatest triumphs and named the achievement the Impregnable Quadrilateral. Now the feat is called the Grand Slam. In 1930, the Grand Slam consisted of the US Amateur, the US Open, the British Open, and the British Amateur tournaments. After achieving the Grand Slam, Bobby retired from competitive golf at the age of thirty and later founded the Masters Golf Tournament, which became one of the four majors along with the US Open, the British Open, and the PGA Championship.

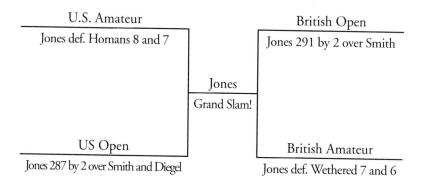

Bobby Jones 1930 Grand Slam of Golf

U.S. Amateur
Jones def. Homans 8 and 7

British Open
Jones 291 by 2 over Smith

Jones
Grand Slam!

US Open
Jones 287 by 2 over Smith and Diegel

British Amateur
Jones def. Wethered 7 and 6

Just as the golf Grand Slam consists of four major tournaments, there are four key principles that every person needs to understand about salvation. First, you are wonderfully and uniquely made (Psalm 139:14) by God, and God created a unique plan (Jeremiah 29:11) for your life so that you can enjoy his special blessings. The unique plan doesn't mean everything that happens to us will be wonderful and that we will live without problems.

Second, each person is separated from God from the first time that he or she consciously breaks one of the Ten Commandments. Each person inherits a sinful nature at birth (Psalm 51:5) and is destined to commit his or her first sin at an early age, which separates us from God. Everyone who has ever lived has experienced this sinful separation from God (Romans 3:23), and if we don't do something about it, spiritual death (Romans 6:23) will be the end.

Third, God loved us so much in spite of our shortcomings that even while we were sinners (Romans 5:8), he sent Jesus to be the bridge over the chasm of sin that separates us from God. Jesus even bore our sin in his body when he went to the cross (1 Peter 2:24). But the good news that we celebrate every day is that Jesus left the tomb and came back to life (Matthew 28:6).

The great news is that, unlike having to win each of the four legs of the golf Grand Slam, God already took care of the first three legs of heaven's Grand Slam. You only need to achieve the fourth and final leg to win heaven's Grand Slam. You must make the decision to exchange your sinful life for a new life in Christ. You must repent, or turn from your sinful life, and ask God to forgive you (1 John 1:9). After you repent, you must trust and accept God's gift of grace to receive eternal life (Ephesians 2:8). By placing your faith in Jesus Christ, you admit once and for all that you cannot earn God's grace and that salvation only comes through Jesus Christ (John 3:16). Then grow in Christ and obedience to God by praying frequently and studying his Word daily. This next sentence is important. Put Christ first in *all* aspects of your life (Proverbs 3:6) so that he will become your Lord.

God offers everyone his free gift of grace. You can pray to receive Jesus Christ into your life as your Savior. Your attitude and change of heart is more important than these exact words.

Prayer: "Lord Jesus, I need you. Thank you for suffering on the cross and dying for my sins. I want my life to change. Please forgive all of my sins through Christ's blood that was spilled for me. Jesus, I ask you to come into my heart. Thank you for your free gift of grace and eternal life with you in heaven. Thank you for the Holy Spirit that helps me any time of the night or day. May I grow in obedience and Christlikeness through prayer and Bible study. Thank you for accepting me as a child in the family of God. In the precious name of Jesus I pray. Amen."

Now consider these statements carefully. You cannot receive Jesus without admitting your sins and vowing to turn away from your sinful life. If you understand each statement and really want to commit to each, you should pray and ask Christ into your heart in your own words. Write your name under *Saint*. You should receive the Holy Spirit and eternal life through Jesus Christ if you were sincere and understood your commitment.

Heaven's Grand Slam

Step 1) God's Plan for Me

Psalm 139:14; Jeremiah 29:11

(Wonderfully Made; Plan for Good)

Step 3) Jesus Died for My Sin

Romans 5:8; 1 Peter 2:24; Matthew 28:6

(Loved sinner; My Sin His Body; Jesus is Risen)

Saint

Step 2) My Sinful Self

Exodus 20:3; Romans 3:23; Romans 6:23

(Self idol; All sinned; Apart from God)

Step 4) Repent, Trust, Obey

1 John 1:9; Eph. 2:8; John 3:16; Prov. 3:5-6

(Cleansed; Grace: Eternal Life; All Your Ways)

Check box if you sincerely intend to:

☐ Repent (turn from) all of your sin.

☐ Trust Jesus Christ as your Savior and Lord.

☐ Obey God by praying and studying his Word.

If you checked all three boxes, pray now for Jesus Christ to come into your heart.

GOLF23:
A RELUCTANT BUT
WISE DECISION

Jonah 3, Romans 8:26

And the word of the Lord came to Jonah, the second time, saying, "Arise, go to Ninevah, that great city, and preach to it the preaching that I bid you."

Jonah 3:1–2

My coaching friend and golf buddy, A. G., shared this gem with me. A. G. coached high school basketball and golf for thirty years, but he had never been fortunate enough to hang a Georgia High School Association banner in his gym for either a state champion or runner-up team. His boys' golf team was locked in a tight battle for second place, and he wanted to hang a banner in what could possibly be his final competition "more than he could describe," he told me.

One of his players finished his afternoon round and told A. G. that he had shot 76. A. G. reminded him to check his scorecard and turn it in. Under the rules of golf, turning in the scorecard ended the player's responsibility. He headed to the scorer's table, and A. G. waited for his last two golfers to finish.

A few minutes later, another player came over and told A. G. that the player who shot 76 was on the board for a 74. A. G. went to the scorer's table and told the GHSA official that he thought there was a problem. The GHSA official pulled his card, and sure enough, it was a 76. A. G. told the GHSA official that "if my team loses because of those two shots, get all the razor blades away from me." Sure enough, his team finished third by two shots.

Looking back, A. G. would love to tell you that he never hesitated, but part of him was screaming, "Don't do it! It's in the rules!" the whole time. But he knew that the kids would *know* every time they came in that gym that the banner was for a mistake. He felt trapped with no good way out. The entire five-hour ride home that night from Jekyll Island, Coach was really down, but he knew that he did the only thing God would permit him to do. There was nowhere to hide and nothing to hide behind, and he knew it.

A. G. believes that God gives kids to coaches so that they have the chance to be good role models in spite of their imperfections because of who he is and who he wants us to be, even though we're not the people that we will be until the day when we are made perfect in Christ. He shared with me that his situation reminded him of Jonah's story. Just as A. G. might have initially been reluctant to go to the scorer's table and deny the 74, Jonah was very reluctant to go to Nineveh and even wound up barfed up on the beach after three days in a whale's belly. But Coach still came through with the right decision, and God still found a way to prompt Jonah to prophesy to the people of Nineveh and save 120,000 people from his wrath.

Prayer: Father God, thank you for the Holy Spirit that prompts us as believers to do the right thing, even when we are torn by our selfish desires to act in another way. In Jesus's holy name, amen.

GOLF24:
THE AUGUSTA
PRESS CONFERENCE

Psalm 7:11–13, Romans 2:1–16, 2 Peter 2:9

The Lord knows how to deliver the godly out of temptations, and to reserve the unjust to the day of judgment to be punished.

2 Peter 2:9

A most unusual event in the history of the Masters was scheduled for the Monday of the 2010 Masters. Tiger Woods held his first press conference that was truly open to the press since his startling allegations of adultery became public. The interview room was jam-packed with more than two hundred golf writers on what is usually a very casual day as golfers get in their first official practice round.

Tiger was introduced by the moderator from Augusta National and answered exactly forty questions over thirty-four minutes from the golf media who had waited anxiously to ask their specific questions. The details and circumstances surrounding Tiger's admitted transgressions were once again chronicled three days before he tackled Augusta National, which is a challenge under any circumstances. Millions renewed their opinions of Tiger amid the fallout that he created for himself.

You had better believe that this press conference was a tough situation. But one day, you could find yourself in a situation that is much tougher and infinitely more important and fearful. That is when you take the stand at the day of judgment. How would any of us answer God's forty most probing questions of our personal lives? Each man and woman passes from this earth and comes before God one on one at the throne of our most holy God.

Unless Jesus takes the microphone from our hands and says, "(Your Name), you can leave now. Well done, good and faithful servant. I will take it from here." That is the beauty of judgment day when you are a believer. Jesus will handle judgment day with God for you, and you will never have to face God. That alone is worth coming to Christ, isn't it? If you are not a believer, one who has earnestly repented and accepted Christ as your Savior, then you are in for one tough press conference. How could a person ever justify and explain to God about the times that he or she has been unfaithful and wasted time chasing the trappings and lures of the world? What a relief it is to know as followers of Christ that Jesus will speak on our behalf at the pearly gates. This type of press conference is inevitable. Prepare now.

Prayer: Father God, thank you for the perfect goodness of your mercy and grace that Jesus can represent me, a sinner washed in the blood of the Lamb. I pray to you now that (my friend) who will face you on judgment day will come to know Jesus Christ as Savior and Lord. In Jesus's name, amen.

GOLF25: ROPE TRICK

James 4:8

Draw near to God, and He will draw near to you.

It is very difficult to get near the best players at Augusta National during the Masters due to the immense crowds, particularly in the last ten years as portions of the course have been cordoned off to give the players more privacy on certain holes such as eight, fifteen, and sixteen. But there are ways to get up close and personal to see your favorite players and follow the leaders on the back nine on Sunday. Here are several techniques that I've learned over the years.

1. Stay half a hole ahead. When the player tees off, you need to be up the fairway near the point where the ball will roll to a stop. Then you have a perfect view of the approach to the green.

2. The rope trick. When people are walking up the fairway ahead of you in the gallery, push against the rope with your thigh. The rope will give about two feet, which is just enough room to pass people on the left. You'll zoom past them like a NASCAR driver on the back straightaway.

3. Wanna get close to your favorite player and on TV? Go to the ball when it goes in the rough. A huge crowd of people will surround the ball, and the marshal will ask everyone

to step back. What you do is put your foot out, stand sideways, and brace yourself. When people start to back up, they will bump into the wedge that you've created, and people will part on your left and right. You'll be on the front row with a perfect view of the action.

Sound like a lot of trouble? It is. You've really got to work hard if you want to see the action. Aren't you glad that we don't have to work that hard to be in intimate contact with God? There is no need to get ahead of him; it works best when we are in step with his perfect timing. We don't have to wait in lines and fight the crowds. Somehow, he is able to handle everybody's needs simultaneously. Want to get close to God? He loves you immeasurably, and he's waiting to meet you right now in the Word or through prayer, which is just plain talking to him. Draw near to God, and he will draw near to you (James 4:8).

Prayer: Dearest holy Father, help me realize that the words don't have to be perfect when I come to you. You just want to spend time with me, and the Holy Spirit will help me with the words. Thank you for being so understanding of my shortcomings. I love you, Father. In the name of Jesus, amen.

GOLF26: PREDICTIONS

Isaiah 53:1

Who has believed our report? And to whom is the arm of the Lord revealed?

One of my favorite golf experiences is to watch the major championships on TV, especially on Sunday. The second major of the year, the US Open, always falls on Father's Day. My wife and daughters have been sweet enough over the years to watch the US Open with me. One of my fondest memories is when the late Jim McKay of ABC would open the telecast with a dramatic welcome to the "Ninety-fifth playing of the United States Open, a national championship conducted by the United States Golf Association."

When you've watched thousands of hours of golf on TV as I have, you begin to learn some of the nuances of the broadcasters. I really get into it and love to predict what will happen next. I will even do some ad lib color commentary of my own. I might see a player trailing by two with four holes to play. He's on a par five playing downwind, and I will mutter, "He needs to make birdie." Two seconds later, the announcer will say, "He needs to make birdie." Allison and Jillian will look at me and say, "Why aren't you doing this?" The wind at Royal Birkdale is whipping into the golfers at thirty miles per hour on a long par 4, and I will say, "He needs to drive it in the fairway to get home in two. " Ditto from the announcer. Perhaps the golfer's iron shot did not produce the distinctive click of a well-struck shot, and I will say, "That needs to get up." Then I get the look from the girls as my echo chimes in.

Just as the announcer occasionally echoed my words, Jesus often repeated the words of the prophets, and particularly Isaiah seemed to be his favorite. Jesus quoted the prophets so that the people of New Testament days could make the connection between his coming as the Messiah and the prophecies from the Old Testament that were shared by Isaiah, Micah, and the authors of the Psalms. The prophets foretold the people what would happen during their day and hundreds of years from now. The evidence of prophecies helps make a strong case for the birth, the miracles, the death, and the resurrection of Jesus Christ.

Prayer: Father God, thank you for the many prophets who foretold the coming of Christ and the details of his death and resurrection. Help me realize that it takes the stories of the prophets to complete the picture that you need us to understand. In the holy and beautiful name of Jesus Christ, our precious Savior and Lord, amen.

GOLF27:
THE RULES OF GOLF

Exodus 20:1–19

You shall have no other gods before me.

Exodus 20:3

Adherence to the rules of golf is essential to the integrity of the game. The rules of golf are determined by the Royal and Ancient Golf Club of St. Andrews and the United States Golf Association. The rules uphold the integrity of the game, and it is up to players to play by those rules strictly or face the consequences of penalties.

Several situations involving violations of the rules of golf stand out. Once, Bobby Jones called a one-stroke penalty on himself when he and he alone saw his ball move after he grounded his club. His comment? "You might as well congratulate me for not robbing a bank." In the 1968 Masters, Roberto De Vicenzo lost the tournament when he signed for a lower score on the seventeenth hole because of a mistake made by his playing partner, Tommy Aaron, who inadvertently wrote down the wrong score. De Vicenzo signed for an incorrect score and was disqualified. His comment? "What a stupid I am!"

God gives us ten rules in the Bible to follow, and when we violate them, we suffer the consequences just like these golfers did. God sent the *Ten* Commandments through Moses from Mount Sinai to give the people of Israel rules for living and obeying him. Ten simple rules for living, and if you break any of them, you're separated from God.

One day, God sent Jesus to be the Savior, the long-awaited Messiah of the people of Israel, and eventually, he also became the Savior of the Gentiles (non-Jews). The reason? No matter how hard we try, we cannot keep the rules that he gave us to live by. So he sent a Savior to atone for our sins, and as believers, we should celebrate the Risen One each day.

Prayer: Thank you, Father, for the Ten Commandments, our rules to live by. May I know the spirit and intent of these rules and use them as my schoolmaster. In Jesus's name, amen.

GOLF28:
ON THE BACK NINE OF LIFE

Hebrews 10:17, Romans 8:1

I will never again remember their sins and lawless deeds.

Hebrews 10:17

The following golf scorecard depicts the average life span. Par is seventy-two, and the average life span is about seventy-two years. Every four years of your life constitutes one hole, so thirty-six years is nine holes. If you're older than thirty-six, do you realize you are on the back nine of life? That should be a sobering thought. I'm fifty-five, so I'm halfway through the back nine. What if you could play number four again when you were age thirteen through sixteen or number eight again when you were age twenty-nine through thirty-two?

If you've gone to pgatour.com to check the tournament leader boards, you'll recognize the color codes. Red is birdie, par is white, but the bluer you get the bigger the mess you made. Here is a typical scorecard of a recreational golfer.

Hole	1	2	3	4	5	6	7	8	9	Out	10	11	12	13	14	15	16	17	18	In	Total
Par	4	5	4	3	5	3	4	4	4	36	4	5	3	4	5	4	4	3	4	36	72
Score	4	6	5	5	4	5	8	6	5	48	4	6	5	5	5	7					

How many of us have ruined a good golf game by losing our cool over one lousy shot? We're still thinking about it four or five holes later as we double bogey ourselves into oblivion. We miss a short putt, and we're looking back three holes later at the green where we missed the short putt. As if that will do any good.

Sometimes we do that with our lives, berating ourselves or wearing ourselves out with guilt and anger over past hurts from fifteen to twenty years ago. We don't ask God for forgiveness so that we can move on, or if we ask God for forgiveness, we don't accept his forgiveness. We ask him and take it back, ask him and take it back again and again, like a broken record.

When we finally realize that Jesus Christ is the only way to find joy and stability in our lives, and we fully repent, and God washes us as pure as snow, guess what the Father does to our scorecard? He wipes away all of our bogeys, double bogeys, and triple bogeys and gives us the Holy Spirit (God in us) for eternity and the free gift of eternal life. He doesn't just forgive; he forgets as if the sin had never happened.

When we get in lock step with him, we're making birdies and eagles and pars the rest of our days until we are made perfect in Jesus Christ. Oh, there will still be mistakes and bogeys and such, but he will turn a triple into a par and a par into an eagle. Because all of our mistakes are forgiven when we turn to the cross, repent, and ask for forgiveness. We are forgiven seventy times seven, and God will forgive us infinitely when we ask him. We are no longer held in condemnation for our sins after we become believers.

Here is your scorecard in Christ after you become a believer.

Hole	1	2	3	4	5	6	7	8	9	Out	10	11	12	13	14	15	16	17	18	In	Total
Par	4	5	4	3	5	3	4	4	4	36	4	5	3	4	5	4	4	3	4	36	72
Score	4	5	4	3	4	3	4	4	4	35	4	5	3	4	5	4	1	2	3	31	66

It's your choice for the next shot for your next hole in life as you decide which club to pull out of your bag. I'm on the fourteenth hole. I've got a hard left-to-right wind, it's uphill, it's late in the day, the sun is in my eyes, and my hands are cold. I've got the bad memories of past failures, such as blocking the shot into the hazard on the right. But I choose to place my trust in Jesus. I hit my tee ball long and straight, stuffed a wedge to three feet, and will sink that birdie putt. I go to the fifteenth hole with a brave new attitude and keep trusting in him. You have a choice too, and I pray to our Almighty God that you decide to pull the right club before your round ends.

Prayer: Father God, help me salvage my life round today no matter what hole I'm on. I repent and take full advantage of your forgiveness. May I truly believe that no matter what sin I have committed, you will forgive and forget. I need to let go of past failures and let you forgive me. In Jesus's name, amen.

SPORTS

S01:
ME, THE PISTOL, AND THE MICK

Ephesians 2:8–9

But by grace you have been saved through faith...

Ephesians 2:8

Two of the greatest players in the history of basketball and baseball respectively were Hall of Famers Pistol Pete Maravich and Mickey Mantle. Pete was perhaps the greatest college basketball player of all time and averaged forty-four points a game at LSU over three seasons, before the three-point line was invented. Pete's amazing ball-handling and passing, which was called *Showtime*, opened the door for future players to execute even more spectacular plays. Mickey was an All-Star centerfielder, played on numerous world championship teams with the New York Yankees, and hit over five hundred home runs despite battling leg problems his entire career. Both players were incredibly popular with fans across the country. Both Pete and Mickey fought the influence of alcohol during their playing careers, finding solace in alcohol to ward off the pressure of gigantic expectations placed upon them by fans, sportswriters, and especially themselves.

But even though both of their lives on this earth were cut short by disease, both had joyous endings for eternity. At age thirty-five, Pete came to a relationship with Jesus Christ two years after he retired from basketball, and he became a prolific evangelist and spokesperson for

God. In 1988, Pete was called up to heaven when he died from a heart attack at age forty in a pickup basketball game in Pasadena, California. In October 1985, less than three years before he died, Pete spoke at a dinner in Phoenix, Arizona, and gave a magnificent testimony. The dinner host and organizer, Jimmy Walker, filmed Pete's talk on a VHS recorder, and bootleg copies of the tape spread across the country over the next fifteen years and eventually wound up on youtube.com (Search "Maravich testimony.") One of those VHS tapes is given credit by former Yankee teammate Bobby Richardson for helping bring Mickey Mantle to a personal relationship with Jesus Christ. Mickey was in his sixties when he watched Pete's testimony just months before he died of cancer. In November 2003, on a Sunday evening, I watched another VHS copy and committed my life to Jesus Christ in my den. What an amazing tapestry God weaves. Some people would say, "Oh, it's a small world," to which I reply, "There is nothing small about God's world." By God's free gift of grace, I will be united with the Pistol and the Mick in heaven.

Prayer: Father God, thank you for the athletic and Christian legacies of the Pistol and the Mick and what each person can learn from them. Thank you for all the people who spread the gospel through electronic media. In Jesus's name, amen.

S02:
THE KEYS TO VICTORY

Romans 7:7–9

I had not known sin, but by the Law…

Romans 7:7

On many sports telecasts, the expert commentator will post the keys to victory during the pre-game show. In basketball, a team must limit turnovers to ten, or prevent a certain player from making three-pointers, or get twenty-five points from the bench. In football, one team must get a hundred yards rushing, or force three turnovers, or score 75 percent of the time in the red zone.

The keys to victory for eternal life have never changed. The three keys are repent, trust, and obey. Repentance is the first key. Repentance means that you are dead serious about *turning away from your sinful life* and *turning toward God*. Pete Maravich once said, "Repentance won't save you, but you can't be saved without it." Simply saying that you want Jesus to come into your heart without giving up your sinful nature won't cut it. Second, you must trust that Jesus Christ died for your sins and believe that he is the only way to heaven. You must believe that he is the Risen One and that he paid the penalty for your past, present, and future sins. There must be no room for the doubt that Satan will try to plant in your mind. Trust means believing beyond a shadow of a doubt that Jesus is your Savior and Lord. Once you have executed the first two keys, in that order, you must love God with all your heart, be obedient to God by praying often, reading Scripture daily, worshiping God through regular church attendance, and being in fellowship with other believers. If you execute on those three keys, you will undoubtedly find victory in Jesus.

Prayer: Father God, thank you for so clearly giving me the keys to victory in Jesus. May I love you with my whole heart and be obedient to you each day. Thank you for loving me unconditionally and more than I can fathom and deserve as a sinner. In Jesus's precious name, amen.

S03:
PLAY TO YOUR STRENGTHS

1 Corinthians 12:4–13

Now there are diversities of gifts, but the same Spirit.

1 Corinthians 12:4

Great athletes and teams play to their strengths. They do what they do best. Coaches analyze the various skills that their players have and design plays to take advantage of their strengths. If a basketball team has great rebounders and fast players, the coach will install a fast-break offense. If a football team has swift, powerful running backs, a veteran offensive line, and a quarterback with an average arm, that team will attempt to run the football the majority of the time. If a tennis player has a powerful serve, the server will charge the net to volley an opponent's weak return.

God made each of us with strengths that we should play to. He also instilled a unique passion within you that you need to find. If, instead of doing the activity that you do best, you try what your friend does, you might be ineffective and become frustrated.

That point applies to our life of service for God. If you are an average singer but an incredibly gifted artist, you should express your love for God through paintings and sketches, not by joining the praise band. Find a way through meditation and prayer or just plain old trial and error to find out what makes your heart beat quickly, and find a way to use that passion for Jesus Christ. Sadly, millions of Christians will live their entire lives without finding the key to serve with joy instead of obligation. Don't become one of them.

Satan loves to see us perform acts for which we have no passion and to do what we aren't cut out to do. I served on a finance team for three years and couldn't stand it. Finance wasn't the bolt of cloth that I was cut from. Satan would love to make you to go to your left, your weaker hand, if you are right-handed.

I realized that I needed to be back in the gym, serving young people, and this change is the most joy that I've received since I began my walk with Christ. Sure, all Christians must perform mundane blocking and tackling, but that's part of being obedient. Nobody gets to live on the mountaintop all of the time. It's what we do in the valley that counts. But mundane activities outside of our passion are not what we think about at night, are not what make our hearts race, and are not what we dream about to help people come to Christ.

Find out what you are great at because everybody is great at something. Look around and see where God is working in that area, and join him. When you do, you will find tremendous joy when you match your passion to God's personal plan for you.

Prayer: Father God, I want to serve you, but it would be really cool if I could serve doing something you have wired me for. Help me find my passion, whether it be sports, music, or mission work, and may I help grow your kingdom for the rest of my days. In Jesus's holy name, amen.

S04:
MEN MAKE MISTAKES
(BUT GOD NEVER DOES)

Psalm 139:14, Jeremiah 29:11, Romans 8:28

I am fearfully and wonderfully made.

Psalm 139:14

Each year, millions of decisions are made in picking youth, high school, college, and pro teams. Mistakes are made all the time in evaluating talent despite highly sophisticated and costly studies. Which great star was cut from his high school basketball team when he was a sophomore? Believe it or not, it was Michael Jordan. Who cuts Michael Jordan? Apparently, a coach did. And what two-time Super Bowl quarterback and two-time NFL MVP was first passed over by the NFL and forced to play in the indoor Arena Football League? Kurt Warner, who led St. Louis and Phoenix to Super Bowls. How many first-round picks have faded into obscurity? Too many to list in this space.

But there is one sure thing you can count on when a person has made a mistake that hurt you or has not placed faith and trust in you. You can count on the unconditional love of God. God has never made a mistake, and he never will because he is perfect and his ways are perfect. You are fearfully and wonderfully made, according to the Scriptures. God knew you before you were formed in your mother's womb. He already had a plan specifically mapped out for your life. That plan doesn't mean you won't have suffering or make plenty of mistakes, but through trust in Christ, you can realize the joy that God wants you to have. God sent his perfect Son who hurt the way you hurt and who personally experienced people making grievous errors in judgment and zealous mistakes when he was crucified on the cross. Through daily prayer, studying the Bible, Christian fellowship, and worship, seek God's plan for your life. Find the inborn passion that is yours and yours alone, and use it to make a difference for eternity in God's kingdom, the kingdom that will never end.

Prayer: Dear Father, I rejoice that you never make mistakes, and you didn't make one when you made me, no matter how short I've fallen. Thank you for forgiving me through Christ's blood that was shed for me on the cross. In Jesus's name, amen.

S05:
THE ULTIMATE SPIKE

Psalm 22:16, Isaiah 53:5–7, 10, Luke 23:32–34

They pierced my hands and feet.

Psalm 22:16

One of the most sensational plays in volleyball is when one teammate sets the ball perfectly near and just above the net and another player drives the ball with the heel of the hand with tremendous force, sending the ball flying into the opponent's court for a point. Players who are the best at performing this high-flying move, called a spike, are in high demand on elite teams. A successful spike that is not returned is called a kill, by the way.

When you hear the word *spike*, let it remind you of the time that Jesus encountered a spike of a very different nature. When Jesus was crucified and placed upon the cross, there were three very large nails or spikes that affixed him to the cross. One spike was driven through both ankles, as was the custom of the Romans during that day, and the other two were driven through each wrist or hand. Before the cross was raised, Jesus was already near death from the awful beating and torment that he had faced when he received the thirty-nine lashes with the cat-of-nine tails, which ripped huge chunks of flesh from his body. A new word had to be invented to describe the incredible pain that men on the cross suffered. That word was *excruciating*, which means "out of the cross."

Yet Jesus loves you so much that he took every minute of six hours to hang, with those spikes driven through his body, to finish off the rule of sin in our lives once and for all. By his wounds we are healed. Six hours is the equivalent of two five-set Olympic volleyball matches, including intermission. Think about how long Jesus hung to make you strong the next time you see a spike.

Prayer: Father God, thank you that Jesus endured the ridicule, the beatings, and the spikes so that I can know the truth that sets me free. In Jesus's name, amen.

S06:
NIGHT LIGHTS

Matthew 5:13–16

Let your light shine, so that men may see your good works and give glory to your Father in Heaven.

Matthew 5:16

The introduction of outdoor lights at Ebbets Fields in Brooklyn in 1938 completely revolutionized professional baseball. Until that time, baseball games could only be played in the daytime. No longer do you read what was once commonplace: "Philadelphia 4, Pittsburgh 3, eight innings, game postponed due to darkness." Night lights opened up baseball to entirely different audiences since students and the working class could not attend games during the day. The revolution that occurred in pro football was the introduction of Monday Night Football in 1970 with Howard Cosell, Don Meredith, and Frank Gifford. Millions of people tuned in to see a game that had never been played regularly on a specific weeknight. Now football games are also routinely played on Thursday nights and Saturday nights. And where would high school football be without Friday night lights? Anyone can see what a vast difference the ability to light a playing field makes.

Just as night lights completely revolutionized sports, the teachings of Jesus completely revolutionized religion and shined the bright Light of good news onto the world of darkness that existed during that day. God can use you and me to shine the light of the gospel in order to revolutionize the lives of our friends living in darkness. When a person receives Christ, he doesn't change his personality or physical makeup. Henrietta Mears, who led thousands of people to Christ through her Sunday school ministry in Southern California, once told a young man, "The lamp didn't destroy its personality when it surrendered to the current. On the contrary—the very thing happened for which the lamp was created; it gave light." The amount of light that you give is proportionate to your willingness to surrender your life to Christ and let him be your sole guide. The stronger your walk is with Christ the greater your glow for him will be. God uses your inner passion and personality along with the Holy Spirit inside you to produce that glow. The brighter the glow the more others will be attracted and will want to know what makes you different.

It's up to you to use some trial and error to figure out what makes your light shine its brightest. I sang a solo once, despite not having any formal training. I must have practiced the song two hundred times in the car. The song was "Spoken For" by MercyMe. I used the crutch of lyrics on a cue card, and by the grace of God, I didn't fall on my face. But several weeks later, I joined our choir and heard a trained soloist, Bob Ellis, sing "Love Divine." I realized my light would shine much brighter coaching young people in the gym than doing something that I had no special talent for. I still sang in the choir, but my solo days were over! You might discover that you are an average athlete but a tremendous actor and singer. You could become a doctor and use your special talents to help people abroad on medical mission trips. You could teach Sunday school if you have a gift for teaching or serve Habitat for Humanity if you have carpentry skills. Discover your inborn talents, develop them, find out where God is working, and use those talents to further his kingdom.

Prayer: Most Holy God, thank you for the passion, abilities, and talents that you gave me at birth. Help me maximize my special talents to shine my light for all to see so that people can see my good works and, as a result, give glory, honor, and praise to you and Jesus. In the holy name of Jesus Christ, I pray. Amen.

S07:
MVP! MVP! MVP!

Romans 12:5–8, John 3:30, Jeremiah 29:11, Colossians 3:17

Plans for welfare and not for harm, to give you a future with hope.

Jeremiah 29:11

You've heard the chant "MVP! MVP! MVP!" for the player whom the fans think is the most valuable player of the game or the season. The MVP, or most valuable player, is typically the player who was the biggest reason that the team did well. It doesn't always mean scoring the most points. It could mean being the best passer or defender in addition to scoring. If a player can lead in such a way that each teammate plays 10 percent better, that improvement can mean the difference in being a champion or being runner-up.

Here is one difference between being an MVP on a winning team and being an MVP for God. God doesn't limit his MVP award to one superstar or super player. He made all of us to be MVPs by creating unique plans for each of our lives. You are an MVP in his kingdom when you use your God-given talents and abilities to make life better for those around you in the name of Christ. You and I are disciples for Christ when we help others know about his great love and tell others how Jesus demonstrated that love on the cross.

God gives us unique gifts and strengths for playing basketball. Some are good rebounders, some are good passers, others can score, and some can play excellent defense. When you discover your strength and use it to benefit the team, you will be most effective. Find out what you are really good at, and do it.

God gives his church members a different array of gifts. The key is for each person to discover the special passion and use it to bring glory and honor to God and the body of Christ, which is your local church. When you discover your gift, through prayer, studying the Word, and following the guidance of the Holy Spirit and use it to help someone else receive Christ, now that is an MVP. When it happens, give God all the glory. Your job is to sow and water, but God draws people to Christ through the Holy Spirit.

Prayer: Dear Lord, may I live my life in a way that makes me an MVP in your kingdom. Keep me humble and obedient when I have an MVP day. Thank you for your perfect and free gift of grace for my salvation, which I do not deserve. In Jesus's precious name, amen.

S08:
SEIZE THE OPPORTUNITY
AND CONVERT

John 3:16–17, 6:44; 2 Corinthians 5:17

For God so loved the world that He gave his only begotten Son, that whosoever believes in Him shall not perish but have everlasting life.

John 3:16

Often in hotly contested games, one play will be the game changer, making the difference between a win and a loss. In football, it could be a fumble deep in your opponent's territory. In lacrosse or soccer, it could be a poor clearing attempt that leads to an easy goal. Perhaps your team has one final possession and needs to convert or score. But, alas, your team fails to convert, and the opponent wins.

There is a much bigger risk in life when you fail to convert. When I was thirteen, a lay speaker delivered a powerful, spirit-filled message on a Sunday morning in my country Methodist church. Despite the tug of the Holy Spirit on my heart, I used my free will to reject the opportunity to repent and trust in Christ. I literally escaped, and outside after the service, I fooled myself into thinking that I would give my heart to Christ the following Sunday. But I didn't realize that I couldn't come to Christ when I wanted, because The Holy Spirit drew me. The book of John says that the Father will draw you to the Son. God tried to draw me to the cross, but I willfully rejected Jesus Christ. That week became a month and then a year, and then, many years later, I found myself far apart from God. It would be thirty-five years before I would come to know Jesus Christ as my Savior. I was very fortunate because I could have been killed in a car crash at seventeen when I fell asleep at the wheel.

You can pray and receive him *now* if you are truly repentant and sick and tired of your sinful life. It's not the words as much as it is the change of heart, the sincere desire to exchange your sinful, wretched life for a new life in Christ. You can pray this prayer and receive Christ as your Savior. "Lord Jesus, I need you. Thank you for suffering and dying on the cross for my sins. Right now, I repent of all my sins and ask you to wash me as clean as snow with the blood of the Lamb, your Son, Jesus Christ, the One who died and rose for me. Now that I am washed clean, Jesus, please come into my heart as my Savior and Lord. Thank you, God, for accepting me into your family as a child of God. Teach me your Word and give me a hunger, and a thirst, and a desire to be obedient to you each day. Direct my path so that I will know your will and your purpose for my life. In Jesus's name, amen." If you sincerely meant that prayer with all your heart, the Holy Spirit is now inside you, waiting to guide your new life.

Prayer: Father God, thank you for never quitting on me. Thank you for the merciful second chances you gave me. Thank you for continuing to woo me to accept your free gift of grace for my salvation through Christ's blood that was shed for my sins on the cross of Calvary. In Jesus's name, amen.

S09:
IS GOD IN THE CENTER
OF YOUR COURT?

Joshua 1:9, James 4:8, 1 Thessalonians 5:18

Have I not commanded you? Be strong and of good courage,
do not be afraid, do not be dismayed, for the Lord your God
is with you wherever you go.

Joshua 1:9

If I mention the sports term center court, it could remind you of
Wimbledon, but that is spelled *Centre* Court. The center court that
I am thinking of is smack dab in the middle of a basketball court,
which is the six-foot radius circle where teams jump center to begin
the game. It's the only time that circle is used during regulation play.
Often, teams barely outline the circle so it doesn't interfere with their
fancy logos painted in the middle of the floor.

That's too bad because the center circle in the court can serve as a
great reminder of our desired relationship with the heavenly Father. If
you are not a believer, it is a certainty that God is not at the center of
your life. If you are a believer, then you should keep God at the center
of your life. You should be very close or in the circle at all times. But
suppose that you have drifted away from God because of unconfessed

sin in your life. The longer this condition lasts the more distant God becomes.

It's not because God has moved away from you. God never leaves the center circle. God never leaves you or forsakes you. God woos each person to a relationship with Jesus Christ. To help that relationship along, God will take 999 steps if you will just take the last one. To God, that's meeting halfway. He already took 999 steps when he sent Jesus to die for you.

But when sin is present in your life, no matter what sin it is—idolatry, hatred, or covetousness—that sin separates you from God. Pretend that God is sitting in the throne in the middle of the center circle of a basketball court. As your separation from him because of sin widens, you take a step back, and then another, and then another until you are completely off the court and out in the parking lot. And then you cry, "God, where are you? I need you." God didn't leave. You did.

Only one thing will restore your relationship with God. Confess the specific sins that have separated you from him and ask for his forgiveness, and he will restore you.

Draw near to God and he will draw near to you. Confessing your sin and asking God to restore you will enable you to recapture the joy that has been sucked out of your life. First Thessalonians 5:18: "Give thanks *in* everything…" You're not supposed to give thanks *for* everything, like going 0 for 10, having six turnovers in a game, or flunking the algebra quiz. But you can give thanks in everything because God is always right there with you when you need him most. Jesus knows your pain at any given moment because he felt that pain at Calvary.

Prayer: Dear Lord, may I keep you at the center of my life today. When I stray, I thank you that you will forgive me and restore me when I confess. In Jesus's beautiful name, amen.

S10:
THE LOCK OF AGES

John 14:26, Ephesians 4:30

Whereby you are sealed to the day of redemption.

Ephesians 4:30

What comes to mind when you hear the term *lock*? Perhaps it reminds you of Locks of Love. People grow their hair long and donate locks for wigs that are presented to cancer survivors. Locks influence every part of our daily lives. Car locks, door locks. House locks, dead bolt locks, and on and on. It was ingrained in my generation to lock your car and take your keys. When did anyone ever not lock their cars?

A lock is also a common sports expression that means a cinch, a gimme, a no-brainer, a guarantee that a certain sports team or sports figure will win. Experts once called Tiger Woods a lock when he took a fifty-four-hole lead into the final day of a major championship. Tiger was 14 of 14 over a twelve-year period, but it was inevitable that some-day he would lose one of those leads to a huge underdog, Y. E. Yang, in the 2009 PGA Championship. In 2007, powerful, undefeated, and number-one-ranked Southern Cal lost a football game at home to Stanford, a forty-one-point underdog. The Soviet Union had the great-est hockey team in the world in 1980 and defeated the Americans 10–3 the week before the Winter Olympics in Lake Placid. But for those of you who remember the semifinal game or saw the movie *Miracle*, you know that the US pulled a stunning upset 4–3. So much for the Soviet lock on that gold medal.

Rest assured that sports contests are subject to surprises and upsets, and you can never count on a sure thing. There is one surefire lock, and it is for eternity. It is an absolute certainty that when you turn away in godly sorrow from your sins that you have committed against God and place your trust in Jesus Christ as your Savior, God will seal you with the Holy Spirit (Ephesians 4:30), claiming you as his child forever. Your transformation will happen in the blink of an eye, and the Holy Spirit will abide in you, guide you, and help transform you as you begin your walk with Christ. Think of the Holy Spirit as God in you. This Holy Spirit will be with you for all eternity.

The fact that the Holy Spirit will abide in you forever when you trust in Christ as your Savior is the lock of the week, the year, and forever. The Holy Trinity is the Rock of Ages and the Lock of Ages. Won't you take advantage of this moment for a surefire lock for eternity?

Prayer: Thank you, awesome Lord, for the Holy Spirit, who locks me down for eternity and keeps Satan from ever stealing my salvation. In Jesus's name, amen.

S11:
I AM FREE!

John 8:32, 2 Timothy 4:2

Then you will know the Truth, and the Truth will set you free.

John 8:32

How can you use your voice to help you score? The idea seems improbable, but often, a teammate cannot see when you shake free from the defense or when you are open near the basket or the goal. One great technique to use is to whoop or shout, "Whoo!" or call a name loudly, "Kevin!" Do you whisper when you want the ball passed to you? Of course not. But do you shout when you aren't open? No. The defense will steal the pass from your team. You shout boldly with perfect timing.

Use the same approach when you tell people about the good news of the gospel. You should be ready for the opportune time to tell a friend or family member how Christ is working in your life. First, you must live your life in a way that you exemplify and honor Christ so that people will see your shining light and the joy in your life, regardless of circumstances. When a person sees you living consistently in Christ, then that person, whether it is a family member, friend, or coworker, one day will ask, "Why are you so cheerful even when things aren't going well?" That situation is a perfect chance to proclaim how Jesus gives you that ability and how he lives in your heart.

If you are a believer, you can't wait to tell people about Jesus. But if you shout it out when a person is not receptive or you are not following the guidance of the Holy Spirit, you could possibly turn that person away from Christ. Knowing when to share and how to share your faith is called discernment. Pray for the person and for the right opportunity to come along. When the right time comes, proclaim Jesus as boldly as shouting for the ball when you are open to make the winning goal.

Prayer: Help me live in a way that honors Christ, and may I have courage, discernment, and wisdom through the Holy Spirit to proclaim your saving grace boldly. In Jesus's holy and precious name, amen.

S12:
THE ULTIMATE SACRIFICE

Isaiah 53:12, 1 Peter 2:24, Psalm 103:12

Who Himself bore our sins in his own body on the tree ...

1 Peter 2:24

In sports contests, you often hear the term *sacrifice*. The word *sacrifice* generally means "to give up something of yourself for others on your team." In baseball, a sacrifice bunt occurs when the batter bunts the ball to advance a runner from first to second, but the batter is not trying to get on base. You can sacrifice an out to advance the runner into scoring position. In basketball, an announcer will lavish praise on the gritty little guard who gives up his body to draw the charge from a hard-charging power forward and prevent a basket. The guard sacrificed his body to help the team. On a football kickoff, a "wedge buster" will sacrifice his body by taking on two or three blockers in the wedge so that his teammates can tackle the kick returner inside the twenty. All of the players in these examples give unselfishly so that their teams will benefit. Each player was "taking one for the team" with his unselfish play.

The ultimate sacrifice of taking one for the team and giving up his body is Jesus Christ. He became the sacrificial Lamb who sought no personal glory but gave the glory to his Father. Jesus figuratively drank from the cup in the garden of Gethsemane and gave up his own body on the cross. Not only did Jesus give up his body, but he carried all of our sins in his own body to the tree (the wooden cross). Jesus went to the cross so that his teammates (you and me) wouldn't be required to. Jesus plowed through the opposition of the Pharisees, Sadducees, Jews, and Romans and was the ultimate wedge buster. He took the charge from Satan, and Jesus's team won the eternal game. Jesus removed our sins from us as far as the east is from the west when God sent his only Son to die for us on the cross, and he defeated death by rising from the grave.

Prayer: Dear Jesus, I can never repay you for sacrificing your body on the cross for me. May I live my life in a way that honors your sacrifice. In Jesus's precious name, amen.

S13:
THE FIRST WORLD CUP

Matthew 26:39–44

Oh my Father, if it be possible, let this cup pass from me, nevertheless not as I will, but as you will.

Matthew 26:42

The World Cup is the most popular sporting event in the world and is held once every four years. The excitement for the event begins to build many months in advance as teams from across the globe seek to qualify for the event. Over a billion people watch the World Cup telecasts in more than two hundred countries. The sport of soccer is popular in the United States, but other sports such as baseball, football, and basketball tend to grab our attention more than soccer. But in most countries, particularly in Europe and South America, a country's national team winning the World Cup is cause for nationwide celebration. The first World Cup was held in 1930 with the little country of Uruguay claiming victory over Argentina 4–2. Uruguay scored three goals using their own soccer ball in the second half.

But did you know there was another world cup almost two thousand years ago, long before soccer was invented? This world cup was held by Jesus Christ in the garden of Gethsemane. Jesus agonized over his final day on earth and what he knew would be an excruciating, painful death on the cross. He tried to prepare the twelve disciples for his death, but they just couldn't fathom what Jesus meant when he said the temple would be destroyed and would rise up on the third day. Jesus had known that Judas Escariot, the disciple who received the dipped bread from Jesus in the upper room, would betray him with a kiss. As Jesus struggled mightily with Satan in the garden, he prayed three times to his Father, "Let this cup pass from me…not My will, but Thy will be done." In God's will being done, Jesus meant that he would follow through and die on the cross to fulfill the Scriptures. He would drink from the cup so that the sins of everyone who would ever live could have their debts paid for their sins. In a sense, Jesus drank from the cup for everyone in this world, the cup for the world, the world cup. The world cup at communion represents forgiveness of sins and eternal life in heaven for anyone who believes in the Savior.

Prayer: Dear Jesus, thank you for drinking from the cup for the entire world to fulfill the prophecies of the Old Testament that promised us you, our Messiah and Savior. In Jesus's holy name, amen.

S14:
THE GREATEST GIFT YOU'VE EVER RECEIVED

Matthew 16:26

For what profit is it to a man if he gains the whole world, and loses his own soul? Or what will a man give in exchange for his soul?

What is the coolest gift you can ever remember receiving, one that made you so happy that you literally bounced around with glee and couldn't put it down? Think back to special birthdays and Christmases.

One special gift that I recall was a set of new golf clubs for my tenth birthday. It was a Johnny Palmer set (no relation to Arnold Palmer) with two woods, four irons, and a putter. I also received some new golf balls and a pull cart. I remember rolling the cart down the street with pride to the vacant baseball field about two blocks from my house. My friend, Darryl, and I hit shots with the clubs that afternoon on a warm, cloudy day. Now I could play out of my bag, and I was on my way. That day brought me a great sense of happiness. But five years later, those golf clubs were on a back shelf. I bought new clubs because the old clubs were too small and outdated.

The second gift that I vividly recall was my 1968 Mustang. The car was a gift from my father and mother in the spring of my senior year in high school. I still remember the smell of the Freon from the air conditioner. What a great treat to have air conditioning in a car—my car! I was so happy and proud to drive that car to school the next day. Now I had the freedom to go wherever I wanted in style. But six months later, that car was a mangled, twisted heap of steel after I fell asleep at the wheel. Shortly after midnight, the car flipped and overturned several times before it came to rest upside down in a culvert. By the grace of God, who had a plan for my life and wasn't quite done with me, I escaped from the car unharmed.

Another moment of happiness came at my apartment at the University of Georgia when a girl delivered a partially torn FedEx package that had been mistakenly delivered to her apartment. There was my custom-made New Orleans Jazz white home jersey with a purple 7 and "Pistol" on the back, just like the one that my idol, Pete Maravich, wore. The jersey would announce what a big Pistol Pete fan I was. I wore the jersey that evening when I played in an intramural basketball tournament, which took a lot of gall. I took more charges that evening than any game that I can remember. I wore the jersey to the NCAA finals in Atlanta several weeks later. Joe Dean, Sr., an LSU legend who knew Pete very well, saw me coming and said in his Louisiana drawl, "Jazz! That's great!" Frankly, he made my weekend. I still have that jersey. In fact, it's been in my closet now for over thirty years. I never knew that it would serve as a constant reminder that God was trying to woo me to a relationship with Christ.

Whether it's golf clubs, a favorite car, or a favorite jersey, all worldly gifts will rust and fade. If you have already determined that your free gift of grace in Jesus Christ is the greatest gift that you ever received, you've got the right perspective. My former pastor Steve Lyle preached often that God's love is so enormous that if you were the only person on earth, Christ would have come down from heaven so that you could have this free gift of grace. Not only do you receive the free gift of eternal life, but you also receive the Holy Spirit to help you with your daily problems. Plus you get to enjoy the brotherhood of fellow believers. The greatest gift is the personal relationship with Jesus Christ, and the blessings that we receive are priceless when we serve him, worship him, and grow in Christlikeness.

Living the Christian life means that you won't be able to accept some gifts that people offer you, especially the ones that feed your sinful nature. But God replaces those missing gifts with gifts far greater, including the joy that comes only from a personal relationship with Christ. Eight months before he died, Pete Maravich told thirty-five thousand people at a Billy Graham crusade, "I wouldn't trade my position in Christ for a thousand NBA championships, a thousand Hall of Fame rings, or a hundred billion dollars. There's *nothing* like the joy of Jesus Christ in your life!"

Prayer: Dear Lord, thank you for the eternal gifts that never rust nor fade and your free gift of grace that brings eternal life, joy, the Holy Spirit, and Jesus Christ, who died for me. In Jesus's holy and precious name, amen.

S15:
HEAVEN'S FINAL FOUR
(LACROSSE)

Jeremiah 29:11; Romans 3:23, 5:8–9; 1 John 1:9; John 3:16

God showed us his great love for us in this way. Christ died
for us while we were still sinners.

Romans 5:8

Our youth indoor lacrosse players at Mt. Zion are fairly new to the
game, so I told them about the 2009 NCAA Men's Lacrosse Final Four
played on Memorial Day weekend. Duke, Virginia, Cornell, and pe-
rennial power Syracuse were the Final Four teams, and Cornell and
Syracuse made the finals that were played before forty thousand fans
in Foxboro, Massachusetts. The final was especially dramatic. Cornell
had a comfortable three-goal lead with four minutes to play and merely needed to maintain possession and avoid mistakes. But Syracuse
fought back with two quick goals. With just a few seconds remaining,
a Cornell player was stripped of the ball, and a desperation pass found
its way onto the cross of a Syracuse attacker. He passed it to Syracuse's
best player, who dove headlong and fired a shot past the Cornell goalie
to tie the game. Syracuse scored in sudden-death overtime to claim
the title. It was a heartbreaking loss for the upstart Cornell team and a
dramatic victory and championship for Syracuse.

There is another final four that you need to understand. First, God created a unique plan for your life so that you can enjoy his special blessings. God blessed you with a special passion that he wants you to use to help him grow the kingdom of God. Second, each person experiences separation from God when he or she gives into temptation and breaks one of the Ten Commandments, the rules that God gave his people to live by. Sin is choosing your selfish way instead of God's way. It is a sin when you disobey your parents, or tell a lie, or steal, or cheat, or place yourself, something, or somebody above God. Third, God loves you so much that he sent Jesus to reconnect us with God forever. Jesus and God hate sin, so God sent Jesus to die for our sins so that he could forgive us of our sins. Fourth, you must exchange your sinful life for a new life in Christ. You must repent, or turn from your sinful life, and turn toward Jesus. Ask God to forgive all of your sins, and then ask Jesus Christ to come into your life as your Savior. When you truly repent of your sins and then believe, or trust, in Jesus as your Savior, you will immediately receive God's free gift of grace, which includes eternal life in heaven. Also, the Holy Spirit will come at that moment to reside in your life forever to guide you and help you with your problems.

God offers everyone his free gift of grace. I invite you to pray this prayer to receive Jesus Christ into your life as your Savior. It's your attitude and change of heart more than these exact words.

Prayer: "Lord Jesus, I need you. Thank you for suffering and dying for my sins on the cross. Change my life today. Please forgive all of my sins through your blood that you shed for me. I ask you right now to come into my heart. Thank you for your free gift of grace that brings me eternal life in heaven. Thank you for the Holy Spirit that now lives in me to help me with my daily problems. Give me a hunger and a thirst for your living Word. Father God, thank you for accepting me into your family as your child. In Jesus's holy name, I pray. Amen."

If you earnestly repented and invited Jesus into your life, you are a child of God's eternal kingdom. Now you should pray (talk) with God, read and study the Bible daily, worship him in church on Sundays, and hang with other Christians. After you become a believer, you will still commit sins, but sin will not control your life. You can ask God to cleanse you anew when you confess your sin to him. First John 1:9 says, "If we confess our sins, God is faithful and just, and will forgive us our sins and cleanse us from all unrighteousness." If you invited Jesus into your life, tell someone now so that the person can support you in your new Christian walk.

S16:
WINNING THE TRIPLE CROWN!

Revelation 2:10, 1 Peter 5:4, 2 Timothy 4:8, Philippians 1:6

There is laid up for me the crown of righteousness...

2 Timothy 4:8

In horse racing, the fastest three-year-old horses vie for the Triple Crown each season. If the same horse overcomes tremendous obstacles and wins the Kentucky Derby, the Belmont Stakes, and the Preakness, that horse is designated as a Triple Crown winner. In baseball, the statistical odds are as high as 50 to 1 that one player will win the Triple Crown by leading the league in home runs, batting average, and runs batted in (RBI).

Do you realize that someday you could be a triple crown winner in heaven? Think about how amazing that would be. First, the Bible tells us in Revelation 2:10 that a believer, who is a person that repented of all sin and received Christ as Savior, will receive the crown of life. The crown of life symbolizes that you've defeated death through trust in Jesus and have received eternal life in heaven. Second, 1 Peter 5:4 reveals that you will receive a crown of glory. In heaven, we actually get to share glory with God. The third leg of this triple crown is the crown of righteousness, which means that we can be in right standing with God because Jesus covered our sins through his death on the cross. Second Timothy 4:8 reveals that in heaven, you will be made perfect, as Jesus is perfect. You will be made complete in Christ (Philippians 1:6). Eternal, glorified, and stainless; now there is a triple crown worth striving for.

Prayer: Father God, thank you for the marvelous triple crown I receive after coming to know Jesus as my personal Savior. In Jesus's name, amen.

S17:
INSTANT REPLAY

1 John 1:9

He will forgive our sins, and cleanse us from all unrighteousness.

One of the great inventions in televised sports was instant replay. Today, instant replay seems second nature because the current generation has never known anything but instant replay and highlight reels. When a tremendous pass occurs, or an amazing catch, or a thunderous slam dunk, the play is worth seeing again and again and again. Those replays capture sports history, and it's nice to have the chance to revisit those great moments.

Pro and college football leagues use instant replay to review the calls by the referees and officials. It's very disheartening and frustrating when your team loses on a bad call. Now, when a call is questionable, the referee will review the play to determine if the call was correct. If it was incorrect, the referee reverses the ruling on the field; even that approach has its limitations as we've seen in college football.

Let's consider a different type of instant replay. It's so much fun to replay in your mind the great events that happen to you: when you make a great play, or get an A on a test, or that special someone flashes a beautiful smile your way. But your conscience will replay a bad action or thought again and again, especially when you've sinned against God. You know the moments when you tell a half-truth, cheat, or steal.

You get really quiet, you get that yucky taste in your mouth, and your stomach is queasy. You replay the situation in your mind and realize that you were so rude to your friend. There is only one action to take, and that is to go to God (and the friend) immediately and ask for forgiveness of that specific sin.

What God does next is really cool. After God forgives you, he removes any record of the sin from your lowlight reel and destroys the evidence that the event ever occurred. He keeps the highlight reel and gives you a special crown in heaven, yet he destroys the lowlights when you confess your sins before him. What an awesome God you and I serve.

Prayer: Father God, thank you for my conscience that instantly replays my bad decisions and wrong plays and for the Holy Spirit which further convinces me of wrongdoing so that I will come to you to be restored to right standing. In Jesus's name, amen.

S18:
TOP TEN PLAYS

Exodus 20:1–17, 2 Corinthians 4:18, Mark 8:34–38

We look not at what can be seen, but at what cannot be seen ...

2 Corinthians 4:18

Millions of sports fans wait expectantly each night to see the top ten plays of the day on ESPN. This concept originated on CNN in the 1980s, but ESPN has taken it to an art form. Top Ten Plays of the Day is the video replay of the most spectacular plays of the day from the entire world of sports. For many people, it's an opportunity to see their favorite players and teams and get another temporary thrill from the acrobatic catches, sensational baskets, and unbelievable goals. These plays are the reasons that fans pack arenas and stadiums, screaming their heads off for their favorite teams.

Top Ten Plays brings to mind another top ten, the Ten Commandments. These commandments are the rules that God gave us to live by three thousand years ago. While the top ten plays change every day, the Ten Commandments never change. I wonder how many fans who religiously watch Top Ten Plays can name the Ten Commandments or even half of them. The Ten Commandments are what matter for eternity, and the top ten plays won't matter at all.

I was just like Joe Fan, seeking instant gratification to fill the God-sized hole in my heart, before I came to a personal relationship with my Savior, Jesus Christ. In the blink of an eye, I could name most of the players who were the subjects of Top Ten Plays, but I ignored the Ten Commandments. Since I flipped the field on Satan, the Ten Commandments have taken on a whole new meaning. The top ten plays are still fun, but they seem irrelevant because I have an eternal focus.

The top ten plays are fleeting, here today and gone tomorrow, and provide temporary happiness and brief satisfaction but lead to nowhere.

The Ten Commandments are permanent, lasting, and eternal. When used properly, they can be used to lead a lost soul to eternity in heaven. Which top ten will drive your actions today?

Prayer: Dear Lord, maker of heaven and earth, thank you for the original top ten that teaches us how to live. In Jesus's name, amen.

S19:
IS THAT G IN YOU?

1 John 1:7, Matthew 5:16

Let your light shine before men so that they may see your good works and glorify your Father who is in Heaven.

Matthew 5:16

Sports drinks such as Gatorade and Powerade are a worldwide, multi-billion-dollar business. Gatorade was the first sports drink invented in the mid 1960s. You had to mix Gatorade powder in a cooler of water, and it was pretty nasty-tasting stuff unless you drank it ice cold. You've seen the Gatorade ad campaign. Is that G (Gatorade) in you? Now it's G1 before the game, G2 during the game, and G3 after the game.

Can you believe that my high school basketball team drank real Coca-Cola at halftime for energy? That's *G* as in gross. Talk about bad for you. Gatorade is effective because the liquid replenishes nutrients and electrolytes in your body much faster than water. Michael Jordan certainly put Gatorade on the mainstream map. Commercials depict Gatorade flowing through a mock-up of a human body. Colors such as purple, yellow, red, green, and blue illustrate the impact.

Suppose that it were possible to drink a liquid that would disclose the amount of sin in your body. Who would dare to drink from this cup for all of our sin to be evident to our family and friends? Would the glow of the Holy Spirit be overwhelmed by the darkness of our sin-stained life? In complete obedience to his Father, Jesus drank from the cup in the garden of Gethsemane and said, "Thy will be done." The reason that he dared drink from that cup was that one day you and I could be cleansed of all of our sins through the precious blood of Christ shed on the cross.

Prayer: Dear Father God, give me the courage to drink from the cup and allow you to cleanse me with the blood of Jesus Christ so that I glow for you and let my light shine for all to see. In Jesus's name, amen.

S20:
DO YOU BELIEVE THE
SCOUTING REPORT?

Isaiah 53:1, John 12:38–41

And to whom is the arm of the Lord revealed?

Isaiah 53:1

An often-overlooked, behind-the-scenes event before competitive sporting events is when one team scouts the other team before they play. A team will send an assistant coach or coaches to watch their upcoming opponent play. The scouts will note the tendencies of the other team's players in game situations. The scouts will record the opponent's offensive and defensive formations. After the game, the coaches collect their notes and compile a scouting report that is delivered to the head coach. The head coach will read the scouting report and structure the upcoming practice to address the major points in the scouting report.

In the Bible, the prophet Isaiah talked about a scouting report of another kind. He asked the people who among them believed the scouting report that he had filed on behalf of God. His scouting report revealed that hundreds of years later, Jesus would be rejected by mankind and that he alone would bear our grief, sorrow, and sin. Isaiah even prophesied the manner in which Jesus would die seven hundred years before it happened. Unfortunately, many people of that day and today, even after the prophecy came true, do not believe this report. The report states that Jesus Christ is the only way to the Father and the only way to heaven. Unlike the game scouting reports that are filed by men and are thus flawed and incomplete, Isaiah's scouting report is 100 percent accurate, as are all statements in the Bible that were inspired by our perfect Creator. Not only did Isaiah file scouting reports about what would happen, but many other prophets such as Jeremiah and Ezekiel made similar predictions that came true.

Prayer: Father God, thank you for sending us the advance scouts who documented exactly what would happen in the game that was played at Calvary hundreds of years later. May all men heed their warnings and come to know Christ before it is too late. In Jesus's name, amen.

S21:
PUT ON THE FULL GEAR

Ephesians 6:10–20, Hebrews 13:5, 2 Timothy 4:2

Put on the full armor of God, that you may be able to stand against the wiles of the devil.

Ephesians 6:11

Full-contact lacrosse is a very physical, contact-prone sport, and injuries can happen frequently, especially if you aren't well protected. To keep from getting hurt, the player must put on the proper shoes, shoulder pads, arm pads, elbow pads, a helmet with a facemask, and protective gloves. The player uses the crosse (stick) to shoot and pass and protect himself when an opposing player attempts a check.

In much the same way, you must clothe yourself with spiritual equipment to keep Satan from hurting you and derailing you. The book of Ephesians teaches that the feet (shoes) are to be shod in peace. The helmet represents the protection of salvation. The breastplate (chest protector) represents righteousness. The crosse can be used like a shield, which represents the faith to trust in God. Then you must rest on prayer and the promises of the Holy Bible.

In lacrosse, you must withstand the body blows of your opponents and the ball striking you in the chest or head, which could injure you. You certainly wouldn't play without a helmet, especially if the other players were wearing helmets. So why go up against Satan each day without the protection of salvation and the weapons of prayer and the Word of God, which makes Satan tremble? Believe that God is as close as your fingertips to help you through every situation. He promised that he would never leave nor forsake you. Use your feet shod in peace to go, share the gospel, and advance the kingdom of God. The first two letters of the word *gospel* is "go." The stick is the sword of the Spirit. Just as you open your mouth boldly to shout to your teammates to pass the ball, use your voice to share the good news with urgency whenever you are given an opportunity. Paul reminds us to share Christ with urgency at two times: when you feel like it and when you don't.

Prayer: Father God, help me walk out the front door each morning clothed in the armor of God and fully prepared to do battle with Satan. In the name of our friend and Savior, Jesus, amen.

S22:
SURPRISE?

Matthew 24:35–44

But of the day and hour knows no man ...

Matthew 24:36

The sports world has seen many surprises that no one could predict. An earthquake in San Francisco before the first game of the 1989 World Series was totally unexpected as a shocked nationwide audience watched. The miracle shot by Mykal Riley of Alabama at the 2008 SEC Basketball Tournament before the tornado hit the Georgia Dome was completely out of the blue. Pittsburgh Steeler running back Franco Harris caught a carom at his shoe tops in the 1972 AFC Championship game and tiptoed down the sideline to score the most unforgettable touchdown in NFL history. This play is known as the "Immaculate Reception." Several hours before those events, nobody sat around and said, "Let's go to the stadium but keep an eye on the horizon," or, "Wait 'til you see the play Franco makes at the end of the game. You won't believe it!" No one predicted these startling events.

Thousands of people each day try to figure out the day that Christ will come back. Their efforts are futile because the Bible teaches us that no one knows the hour except the Father. Not even Jesus Christ knows. Now, if Jesus doesn't know, why would you and I spend five seconds trying to figure it out? Twenty-four hours before Christ comes, the world will be as oblivious as the Steeler fans the day that Franco ran for the touchdown.

But rest assured. Christ *is* coming. What do you need to do to get ready? You can feel the earthquake and run for cover. You can feel the tornado hit the Georgia Dome, like my family and I did, and run for cover. But when Christ comes in his power and glory, it will be too late to run for cover. It will be too late to repent. No one will be saved on the day of his arrival by an immaculate redemption. Suppose Christ comes at 4:00 P.M. The clock will suddenly read 00:00. The game of life will be over, and you will be lost for eternity if you have not already placed your trust in Christ. Many Christians believe that recent events point to the end times being near. Come to Christ today while there is still time on the clock.

Prayer: Father God, may I take your warnings seriously and understand my need to repent now. The best time to accept Christ is today. Please change my heart and allow me to receive Christ as my Savior before it is too late. In Jesus's name, amen.

S23:
UNLIKELY HEROES

Luke 19:1–9, Mark 3:14–18, John 4:7–26, Hebrews 11

And he ordained twelve, that they should be with him …

Mark 3:14

Frequently, the most unlikely sports heroes emerge during the biggest contests. During the first Super Bowl, a journeyman receiver named Max McGee came off the bench for the Green Bay Packers after the starting receiver was injured on the first play of the game. McGee caught seven passes and was named the MVP. The unheralded Bucky Dent of the Yankees hit a three-run homer in a playoff game in 1978 against the Boston Red Sox to extend the curse of the Bambino. The unknown Y. E. Yang outplayed Tiger Woods down the stretch in the 2009 PGA Championship to become the first man to defeat Tiger in the final of a major when Tiger led going into the final day.

There have been some unlikely biblical heroes too. Jesus chose a prostitute who had been married five times, a tax collector, and fishermen to help him spread the gospel. The woman at the well couldn't keep quiet about the man that she knew to be the Messiah after Jesus told her everything about herself and promised her living water. Zacchaeus climbed out of the tree, had dinner with Jesus, and excitedly told the people that he had ripped off with excessive taxation that he would pay them back with 400 percent interest. Peter and Andrew abandoned their fishing nets, and though they didn't get it for a long time, eventually, changed the world for Christ.

These folks weren't the religious leaders of the day, nor were they leaders of any kind. But God used them to change the world. You and I are more like the Bible heroes than today's well-spoken spiritual leaders or the talented sports heroes. Most of us have average skills. But God uses ordinary people by giving them supernatural ability through the Holy Spirit. He can use us too if we will only let him.

Prayer: Father God, it is so great that I don't have to be the world's best or a big shot to help you further your kingdom on earth. May I love you more today than yesterday and be obedient to the Lord Jesus. In Jesus's name, I pray. Amen.

S24:
THERE'S GONNA BE
A REVOLUTION

Matthew 5:1–12

Blessed are the meek, for they shall inherit the earth.

Matthew 5:5

Sports fans benefit from changes in rules and equipment that greatly enhance the enjoyment of particular sports. Soccer's rule eleven, the offside rule, was introduced in 1904, and this rule made the sport much more exciting. In basketball, the twenty-four-second clock that was introduced in the NBA in 1954 probably saved the league. The shot clock resulted in much more scoring and more exciting plays, and the NBA grew and signed a national TV contract, taking the sport to another level. In 1985, North Carolina and Virginia, the top two teams in the nation, staged an epic battle for the first thirty minutes of the game until North Carolina held the ball for eight minutes. Madison Avenue eventually said to college basketball, "We're not watching grass grow." In the mid-80s, the introduction of a shot clock, the three-point line, and the expansion of the tournament field to sixty-four teams resulted in a newfound level of interest that eventually led to college basketball's March Madness. In golf, hickory shafts were replaced by steel shafts, which allowed golfers to practice more and hit more reliable shots, and gutta percha balls were replaced with core compression golf balls, which flew further with more consistency. These events took their respective sports to a new level.

Jesus revolutionized the world through his teachings and ultimately changed the course of time by going to the cross to be the final sacrifice that mankind would ever need. The powerful religious leaders who brought attention to themselves by pompous praying in public were rebuked and told to pray in private. When you give, do it in private, and don't let anyone know how much money you gave or else you lose your reward from the Father. The meek will inherit the earth? C'mon, are you serious? Yes, Jesus was dead serious, so serious that he took on the religious leaders of the day and instilled a new way of living based on love for God and for your fellow man. Turning the other cheek and loving your enemies? Yes, the changes that Jesus introduced made the game of life better for all who would believe in him as the Savior of the world.

Prayer: Thank you, Jesus, for your new teachings that revolutionized the world. Thank you for going to the cross so that I could choose to have eternal life. Thank you for your resurrection and ascension to heaven. I will see you on the streets of gold someday. In Jesus's name, amen.

S25:
YOUR UNIQUE GAME PLAN

Jeremiah 29:11–13

I know the plans I have for you, says the Lord ...

Jeremiah 29:11

Every team creates a game plan for an important game. The coaching staff takes input from scouts, watches game film, studies opponents, and creates a strategy to give its team the best possible chance for victory. If you are a member of the team, that game plan is shared thoroughly with you and every other player. Unless the game plan is shared with the team, the player will not understand what offense to run, what defense to execute, and especially what to do in crucial situations.

God creates a life plan for every person that has been born. Unfortunately, millions of people will never know the unique plan that God has created for each of their lives. Do you realize that God has a special plan for your life? It's true. And do you know that you will never know your plan, which is far superior to anything you can create, unless you trust in Jesus Christ as your Savior? You might say, "Oh, I'll have a good life anyway." But that life will end one day, and then what? You might never fulfill the last step of the plan, which is to live for eternity with God and Jesus in heaven. While God has a unique set of steps in each person's plan, the last step is always the same: "Come home and live with Me for eternity." Why not unite with Christ now and realize God's eternal game plan for you?

Prayer: Father God, thank you for loving me so much that you would make me to be different from any person who has lived or will ever live. When you made me, I believe that I came with special instructions so that I could experience the joy of being a Christian in service to you. In Jesus's name, amen.

S26:
RACE TO THE FINISH

Matthew 6:19–21, 28:19–20; 1 Corinthians 9:24–27

I will be with you always, even to the end of the age.

Matthew 28:20

In August 2009, Usain Bolt set two more track world records by running an astounding 9.58 in the 100-meter dash and an astonishing 19.19 in the 200-meter dash. As Paul wrote in 1 Corinthians, only one runner gets the prize in a race, even though all of them have gone through strict training. What does the winner of races like this receive? The winner receives millions of dollars in endorsements and appearance fees, fame, adulation, medals, and trophies. All of these earthly rewards will tarnish and fade, and a generation later, superior athletes will eclipse the records of Bolt in track and field and Michael Phelps in swimming.

Paul teaches us that as Christians, we should not run aimlessly when it comes to advancing the cause of Christianity. Each Christian will receive a crown, and I believe we will receive jewels in the crown for people that we lead to Christ. We should run with purpose, thinking of heaven daily and how God can use us so that our friends and family members, neighbors, coworkers, youth, and children can join us in heaven.

We must develop our minds so that we are transformed to be more like Christ and prove what God's perfect will is. If you don't have an eternal mindset, you will wander aimlessly day after day, thereby forfeiting a crown of salvation that you could receive one joyous day. It is our duty as Christians to run the race with purpose, realizing that it's not a sprint but a marathon, so that we can finish well for Jesus Christ.

Prayer: Father God, help me realize each and every day that I am here for a purpose: to love you, to obey you, and to be filled with a desire to know you more. Show me how to use my talents to help others experience your love. In Jesus's name, amen.

S27:
SAINTS CHEERING IN THE STADIUMS OF HEAVEN

Hebrews 12:1, Philippians 3:14

Therefore, since we are surrounded by such a great cloud of witnesses ...

Hebrews 12:1

The Rose Bowl. Dodger Stadium. Yankee Stadium. Fenway Park. Wembley Stadium. Sanford Stadium. Memorial Coliseum. Olympic Stadium. What a thrill it would be to win a race, or hit a walk-off homer, or score the winning touchdown in an arena like these. Imagine the thrill of hearing a hundred thousand people scream your name in glee. Most of us will never hear such a sound directed toward us. But do you realize that there is great cheering and celebration every day in heaven, rejoicing as one sinner after another is saved? The great cloud of witnesses refers to the angels and saints, hundreds of millions of them according to Revelation. Do the math with me. If ten million people are saved around the globe each year, that's about thirty thousand per day, or one every few seconds. The "salvation scoreboard" is lit up continuously, and the cheering never stops in heaven.

When we sin and stumble and fall in our races each day, there is encouragement and exhortation from above to "Get up!" and finish the race. God doesn't leave us or forsake us when we fall as Christians. Know that your grandparents, parents, and loved ones who have preceded you to heaven are praying for you to finish the race and receive the prize for which God, through Christ Jesus, is calling you up to heaven.

Prayer: Father God, what an awesome revelation it is to realize that there are saints and angels pleading for me and encouraging me in heaven as they sing praises to you. May I remember that the saints are always there for me, and that you will never quit on me. In Jesus's name, amen.

S28:
LIGHT UP THE SCOREBOARD
IN HEAVEN

Luke 15:3–10, John 3:30

There is joy in the presence of the angels of God over one
sinner who repents.

Luke 15:10

When I see kids raise their hands at invitation time at the gym or at
FCA, I can't help but wonder if some of them really have received
Christ. You can be pretty sure when a kid's hand goes straight up immediately that the kid wants Jesus Christ in his or her life. If kids peek
and see a hand go up, they think that they need to raise their hands.
You can be pretty sure that decision won't stick due to a lack of commitment. But what about the kids in the middle? I believe that the
saints and the angels know, and certainly God and Jesus know, who the
Holy Spirit is poured into at that moment.

Remember the fireflies that come out at the beginning of summer?
I called them lightning bugs the first time that I saw them in Alabama.
I captured six or eight in a mayonnaise jar with holes punctured in the
lid. As I started into the house, I stubbed my toe and went sprawling,
skinning my knees as the jar crashed to the sidewalk. Suddenly, those

fireflies were free again. But I have fond memories of five or ten lighting up simultaneously in my grandmother's yard.

I like to imagine that when invitations are given and Christ is truly received in the hearts of young people or older people, that bright lights signal this awesome news to the saints and angels. Why not? If there is great rejoicing when only one sinner comes to Christ, why can't it be put up in lights for the saints to see? With God anything is possible. When a hockey player puts the puck in the net, the red light comes on, the siren goes off, and the fans cheer like crazy. Why wouldn't that happen in heaven? I don't know that it does, but I can surely imagine it. That vision gives me an idea that our efforts to grow God's kingdom count more than we will ever know.

Picture the saints and angels in heaven cheering for that one lost soul that you helped lead to Christ. And the red light comes on in heaven. How cool will that be?

Prayer: Heavenly Father, give me a clear picture that motivates me to do the little things like sowing seeds in fervent hope that I can help lead someone to Christ. In Jesus's precious name, amen.

S29:
GUARD YOUR HEART
(AND YOUR TONGUE)

Psalm 73:3–9, James 3:5–10, Matthew 12:34

But no man can tame the tongue…it is full of deadly poison.

James 3:8

It was an interesting week in the fall of 2009 under the white-hot lights of politics and entertainment. A Caucasian congressman shouted at our African American president, "You lie!" A female African American tennis star berated a female Asian American line judge at the US Open. An African American male musician told a young Caucasian female star that she did not deserve to win a music award. Anger knows no age, gender, or racial boundaries.

Now you and I messed up that same week. But the difference is that our events played out in obscurity in the privacy of our homes, schools, workplaces, and churches. The tongue weighs a few ounces, but the damage it does cannot be measured. The Bible assures us in Romans 6:23 that sin is sin, and the wages of sin is death. All sin is an affront to God. But here is the lesson to be learned. If you are in the public eye or in the eyes of others at school, at work, or at church, it only takes an instant, one slip of the tongue, to cancel years of trust and goodwill. Your reputation can be ruined.

You and I should thank God every day for his mercy, that we don't receive the full measure we deserve for the times we have committed sinful acts. But they won't go unpunished forever for the unrighteous. Psalm 73 assures us that the unrighteous will receive their punishment, for we serve a just God who does not turn his back on any sin, large or small. Neither does Christ. Christ hated sin but loved us so much that he died for our sins so that we could be forgiven.

Isn't it interesting that you can wiggle your tongue like a snake sliding on its belly? Snake as in the serpent in the garden of Eden. We cannot control the slippery tongue no matter how hard we try, but the good news is that there is forgiveness from God awaiting us immediately after we confess our sin to him.

When your heart is right with God, you will be able to catch yourself much more often before you say something you never thought you would say. You would instantly give anything to have those words back. You desperately want to erase the slip that makes people say, "He said that? And he's supposed to be a Christian!" Train your mind daily, and guard your heart with the Word of God so that the overflow of your heart is kindness, compassion, love, and peace.

Prayer: Father God, I know that only one person has ever failed to shout out in unrighteous anger, and that is Jesus. Help me live so that I minimize those times that I sully my reputation as a Christian and bring dishonor to the name of Christ. Help me guard my mind with your holy Word and prayer so that I can be in right living with you. In Jesus's name, amen.

S30:
SIGNED, SEALED, DELIVERED—
YOU'RE MINE!

Ephesians 4:30, Romans 8:1

Let there be no condemnation, for all which are in Christ
Jesus...

Romans 8:1

Dr. Michael Youssef, the senior pastor at the Church of the Apostles
and the founder of Leading The Way ministry, once delivered a wonderful sermon on how God stamps his believers with the seal of the
Holy Spirit. He described how the gigantic cedars of Lebanon were
cut down and stamped with a special seal to let everyone know that
this was not just any cedar but one of the hallowed cedars of Lebanon.
Those cedars were special because they were used to build Solomon's
Palace and the Temple of Jerusalem. Those cedars were clearly designated that they came from a special place before they were delivered.

Here is the joy that you can receive today. Once you have been
cleansed for the first time with the blood of our precious Savior, Jesus
Christ, God performs a special closing ceremony. God seals you with a
person, the Holy Spirit, who comes into your being forever. God proclaims, "Satan, this child is mine! You can never take away my child's
salvation and free gift of eternal life with me in heaven. This is my

child, who will never darken the gates of hell." MercyMe's hit song "Spoken For" proclaims, "Covered by your Love Divine, child of the Risen Lord. To hear you say this one's mine, my heart is spoken for."

When you became a child of God, you were spoken for, and he sealed you with the Holy Spirit. He signed for you with the precious blood of Christ. He delivered you from the dominion and bondage of sin. "Signed, sealed, delivered"—you're mine!

Prayer: Father God, may I experience the joy of knowing beyond a shadow of doubt that I have been signed, sealed, and delivered by you through the precious blood of Christ. In Jesus's name, amen.

S31:
TIME!

Psalm 90:4, 2 Peter 3:8

For a thousand years in your sight are but as yesterday…

Psalm 90:4

Each major sport, with the exception of baseball, has a distinct component of time. There is a specific beginning and end. High school basketball consists of four quarters of eight minutes with allowance for overtime after regulation time ends in a tie. Soccer has two forty-five-minute halves with allowance for injury time. Nobody is ever quite sure when the soccer game will end. Only the person keeping injury time knows. High school football has four twelve-minute periods with allowance for extra time during playoffs. College football allows for extra overtime, but it's not timed. Pro football has a sudden-death overtime period that ends when the first team scores. All of the timed sports allow for stoppages of time during games. It's all very confusing to the novice.

Years ago, sports clocks only had a minute hand and second hand. When clocks went digital, the actual number of minutes and seconds could be displayed. Clocks became even more precise and allowed for a tenth of a second to be displayed during the last minute of basketball games. Swimmers are timed to the hundredth of a second. Recall that Michael Phelps dove for the wall and claimed a gold medal at the

Beijing Olympics by one one hundredth of a second. World records and the outcome of sports contests are occasionally determined by the blink of an eye.

But God is not time bound, nor is he space bound. God invented time as a dimension for the earth and its inhabitants. We make ourselves crazy making adjustments of this precious commodity called time, which is limited on earth. There is a specific start time (birth) and an end time (death) for each person. Everyone is subject to the limitations of time with no exceptions.

But there is no concept of time in eternity. Eternity implies there is no end. Your existence will be for eternity in heaven or hell after this worldly life ends. To God, a thousand years is as a night watch. Think about this point. The average person's age is about forty years old, which means he or she has on average about fifteen hundred more weekends to spend on this earth. Many people would say, "Fifteen hundred weekends? I've got plenty of time to have my fun before it matters." But God doesn't give you fifteen hundred weekends at once. He gives you today, one day at a time. He gives you one day at a time to live, and it is up to each of us to live the day fully for him. You live it out of love and obedience for the One who made you and the One who came to earth as a baby to save us. Jesus came expressly to die for your sins so that you can experience what it means to live beyond the dimensions of time and space *with God*, to live in paradise and not in exile. When you receive Christ, you receive a one-way ticket beyond time and space to a glorious homecoming with God. Is it time that you secured your future?

Prayer: Father God, thank you for giving us time that helps us be where we are supposed to be. But I want more than time. I want eternity with you, where there are no limitations of time and space. Please prepare me to share my hope of a glorious reunion with you. In Jesus's name, amen.

S32:
WHAT A SAVE!

John 3:1–7, 2 Corinthians 5:17, 1 Peter 1:23

He is not the same anymore, a new life has begun!

2 Corinthians 5:17

One of the most thrilling plays in a soccer game is when the goalkeeper uses super-quick reflexes to prevent the ball from going into the net for a score. The ability of the goalie to deflect and catch balls often means the difference between winning and losing the game.

Please know there is a different type of save that is much more important. Instead of happening thousands of times over the course of years, as happens with an experienced goalie in practice or games, this type of save happens only once for a person. When Nicodemus asked Jesus what he must do to be reborn, Jesus explained to him that only through faith in me could he be reborn, born again, or saved. This reply greatly puzzled Nicodemus. What did Jesus mean, being born again? How could he, as a grown man, be born for the second time?

But a second birth, a spiritual birth, is exactly what Jesus meant. You are born physically once as a boy or girl. Then, when you repent of your sins and trust in Jesus as your Savior, you will be born for the second time, this time spiritually. Physical birth, then spiritual birth. Born twice, die once. If you aren't saved, you will be born once and die twice (a physical death and spiritual death).

This spiritual birth *saves* you from eternity spent in hell. It is true as the hockey fan's sign once read: "Jesus saves!" When someone is reborn spiritually, that person becomes a new person inside and is not the same anymore. A new life has begun.

Prayer: Dear Father in heaven, thank you for your gift of Jesus Christ, whom I can learn from in the Bible, and that it is possible for any person to experience what it means to be born again. In Jesus's name, amen.

S33:
THE ULTIMATE ASSIST

Luke 2:10–12, John 14:26

But the Comforter, which is the Holy Spirit, whom the Father
will send in my name …

John 14:26

The beauty of sports is most evident when a team executes beautifully
timed passes that result in a score. A perfect corner kick is headed into
the goal by a diving striker. A quarterback arches a long bomb down
the sideline to a streaking receiver in the corner of the end zone. A
shortstop goes behind second and flips to the second baseman, who
hurls a relay to first just in time. In hockey, the center flips a pass to
the right wing, who fires a shot deflected into the goal by the left wing.
In lacrosse, it's a well-timed pass from behind the goal to a player who
catches and fires in one motion into the goal for a score. My favorite
pass is in basketball, when a player throws an alley oop to a streaking
forward for a thunderous slam dunk.

In many sports, an assist is awarded to the person who makes the
pass that sets up the basket. In hockey, two assists can be awarded for
one goal. The player who passes to the player who passes to the goal
scorer is also awarded an assist. The assist is a great statistic because it
gives credit among teammates other than the goal scorer.

So where do God and Jesus come into the assist picture? Well, the best two assists that I can recall involved God and Jesus. First, God sent, or passed, Jesus from heaven to earth, where Jesus was born in a manger. Without that eternal assist from God, our hope for eternity would be completely different. Second, Jesus returned the favor by sending, or passing, the Comforter or Holy Spirit to the disciples after his ascension to heaven forty days after his resurrection. This Comforter or Helper is the same Holy Spirit that descended upon Jesus like a dove after John the Baptist baptized Jesus in the Jordan River.

The next time you see a great pass or series of passes, and you can see the happiness on the faces in the crowd, think of the greatest combination of all time. No, it's not Stockton to Malone, or Magic to Abdul-Jabbar, or even Jeter to Cano to Teixeira. It's the perfect timing of God to Jesus to the Holy Spirit.

Prayer: Thank you, Father God, for the greatest combo that has ever passed us love, mercy, and grace. You, Jesus, and the Holy Spirit brighten our daily lives and make our lives worth living. In the name of Jesus Christ, amen.

S34:
THE REST IS UP TO YOU

Romans 12:2

Do not be conformed to this world, but be transformed by
the renewing of your mind, such that you may prove what is
that good and acceptable and perfect will of God.

You can be taught how to ride a bicycle. You can be taught the proper
way to hold a golf club. You can be taught how to hold a tennis racket.
You can be taught how to hold a basketball or baseball. But eventually,
you must swing the club, or hit the tennis ball, or shoot the basketball,
or throw the baseball in order to be successful. If you attempt to learn
without proper instruction, you will pick up bad habits that are very
difficult to correct. Most kids who shoot a basketball the wrong way at
eight or nine years old will never develop proper technique. No matter
how much coaching you receive or how many camps you attend, you
still must play the game. No one can play the game for you.

   You can be given a Bible, but it's up to you to use it or it will collect dust on your shelf. You can be told the benefits of prayer, but you
will never receive the benefits unless you go to God and start talking to
him. You can be told that you need to be part of youth group to grow
in Christ, but eventually, it's up to you to have the courage to walk
through the door. Just as coaches are well-meaning in giving you sports
instructions, so are Sunday school teachers, youth counselors, pastors,
and parents. These folks have a wealth of experience and desperately

want to impart to you the goodness and wisdom that God has given them.

Heed their calls, follow their advice, and draw closer to God. The benefits are out of this world.

Prayer: Thank you for my coaches who teach me to play sports better and for my teachers who teach me to transform my mind to be like Christ. May I do the same coaching and teaching for others. In Jesus's name, amen.

VERSES BY BOOK

1 Corinthians

2:1–5	FB10
3:9–15	FB20
6:18–20	FB15
9:22	BB13, FB11
9:24–25	FB10
9:24–27	BB02, S26
12:4	S03

1 John

1:7	BB15, BK32, FB03, S19
1:9	BB15, BK18, Golf03, Golf22, S15, S17
3:17	FB01
5:21	FB13, BK10

1 Peter

1:23	S32
2:24	BB15, S12
5:4	S16
5:7	BB14

1 Samuel

12:1–12	Golf08

1 Thessalonians

4:13–17	FB16
5:18	S09

1 Timothy

4:12	BB02

1 Chronicles

4:9–10	FB22

2 Corinthians

4:18	FB16, FB17, S18
5:17	BK18, FB02, FB11, Golf06, Golf21, S08, S32
5:17–20	BB06
12:6–9	BB01

2 Peter

2:9	FB18, Golf24
3:8	S31

2 Samuel

9:1–13	BK03

2 Timothy

3:16	FB12
4:2	S11, S21
4:7	Golf12
4:8	S16

Acts

1:1–8	BK08
2:1–17	BK17
5:1–5	FB24
26:4–5	BK33

Colossians

3:17	BK22, FB20, Golf01, S07
3:23	BB25

Daniel

9:25	FB09

Deuteronomy

31:6	BK24

Ecclesiastes

2:11	BK28

Ephesians

2:8	Golf22
2:8–9	S01
4:30	S10, S30
5:20	Golf18
6:10–20	S21

Exodus

20:1–17	BB05, BK31, FB03, S18
20:1–19	Golf27
20:4–6	BK17

Ezekiel

36:26	FB23

Galatians

3:24	BK31, BK32
3:24–29	BB21
4:4	FB09
6:9	BK07

Genesis

39:7–21	FB15

Habakkuk

3:18–19	BB23

Hebrews

1:12	BK11
4:16	FB21
10:17	BB16, BK01, BK21, Golf20
11	S23
12:1	BK23, S27
12:2	BK05, BK26
13:5	BK24, S21
13:8	BK11

Isaiah

7:14	FB14
9:6	FB14
45:5	FB13
45:22	FB13, FB32
50:7	Golf07
53:1	Golf26, S20
53:1–5	BK25
53:5	Golf11
53:5–7	S05
53:10	S05
53:12	S12
55:8–9	FB25

James

1:17	BK11
1:26	BB14
2:17	BB11, BB26
3:5–10	S29
4:8	BK24, Golf25, S09
4:14	BK05
4:14–15	FB11

Jeremiah

1:5–6	FB23
6:16	Golf05
29:11	BB15, BB17, FB27, Golf22, S04. S07, S15, S16
29:11–13	S25
29:13	BB17, Golf19

Job

38	BB07

John

3:1–7	S32
3:16	BB15, FB04, Golf15, Golf22
3:16–17	Golf06, S08
3:30	BB26, S07, S28
4:7–26	FB04, S23
6:44	FB24, S08
8:32	BB18, Golf03, S11
10:10	FB22
11:25–26	BK18, Golf14
12:38–41	S20
14:6	BB05, BB10, BB12, BB19, BK12, BK18, BK21, Golf02

14:26	BK08, S10, S33
15:5	FB30, Golf10
15:12	FB01

Jonah

3	Golf23

Joshua

1:8	BK31, FB17
1:9	BB09, BB21, BK24, S09

Lamentations

3:22–23	BB18, Golf28
3:22–26	BK13
3:32	BK13

Luke

2:10–12	S34
2:10–16	FB14
9:62	BK27
12:40	BK20, BK23
15:3–10	S28
15:10	FB06
19:1–9	S23
23:32–34	BK25, S05

Mark

1:15	BK09
3:14–18	S23
8:34–38	BB08, S18
9:35	BK02
12:30–31	FB01
15:25–37	BK14

Matthew

3:1	FB23
4:17	BK09, FB23
5:1–12	S24
5:13–16	S06
5:16	S19
5:23–28	FB15
5:48	BB04
6:19–21	S26
6:30	FB24
7:1–5	BB07
7:7	FB17, FB22
7:13	Golf02
7:21–29	BK19
7:23	BK30
7:24–27	FB05
9:37–38	BK16
12:34	BB14, S29
16:26	BB08, S14
24:35–44	S22
25:32	Golf02
25:40	FB01
26:36–44	FB08
26:39–44	S13
27:32–50	FB01
27:51	FB21
28:1–9	Golf06
28:19–20	BK16, S26

Micah

5:2	FB14

Nehemiah

2:5	FB09

Philippians

1:6	BB04, BB22, BK13, FB19, FB31, S16
1:20–21	BK05, BK15
3:11–14	FB07
3:13–14	BB02
3:14	FB10, S27
4:13	BK03, FB26, Golf01
4:19	FB17

Proverbs

3:5–6	FB29
27:17	Golf04

Psalms

7:11–13	FB18, Golf24
12:6–7	FB12
19:12	BB04
22:16	BK25, S05
37:4	FB28
51:4	Golf08
51:10	BB04
62:6–7	FB05
73:3–9	S29
90:4	S31
103:12	BK01, S12
119:105	Golf05
121:1–2	BB27
139:14	BB15, Golf22, S04

Revelation

1:8–13	FB20
2:10	S16
3:20	BB13, FB02
5:11	FB06
20:15	BB03
21:1–5	FB16
21:27	BB03

Romans

2:1–16	FB18, Golf24
2:6–10	BK07
3:23	BK10, FB13, S16
5:8	BB15, Golf13, Golf22
5:8–9	S15
6:23	BB05, BB15, Golf09, S09
7:7–9	S02
8:1	Golf20, S30
8:18	FB16
8:26	BK06, BK08, BK29, Golf23
8:28	FB06, S04
10:8–13	BB24
12:1–2	BK21
12:2	BB04, BK21, BK22, FB04, S34
12:3–8	BK04
12:5–8	S07
12:12	Golf17

Titus

3:5	FB02

INDEX

A

B

H

I

J

James, Lebron	BK10
Jesus Christ, Birth of	FB14
Jesus Christ, cleansed by blood of	BK32, Golf22, S08, S15, S19
Jesus Christ, died for our sins	BK01, FB08, FB13
Jesus Christ, focus on	BK26
Jesus Christ, Gethsemane	FB08, S13, S19
Jesus Christ, knowing	BK30
Jesus Christ, sacrifice of	S12
Jesus Christ, second coming of	FB16, S22
Jesus Christ, teachings of	S24
Johnson, Eddie	BK15
Johnson, Magic	BK04
Johnson, Zach	Golf04, Golf11
Jones, Bobby	Golf22, Golf27
Jones, Julio	FB07
Jordan, Michael	S04, S19
judging others	BB07
Judgment Day	BK19, FB18, Golf24

K

Keeler, O. B.	Golf22
Koufax, Sandy	BB08
Krauss, Barry	FB08

L

Langer, Bernhard	Golf09
Lanier, Stanton	FB31
laughter	BB23
legacy	BK06, BK12, FB30, Golf12, Golf13
Lehman, Tom	Golf16
light unto my path	Golf07

M

N

O

obedience	BB22, BK27, FB22, S19
Oher, Michael	FB01
Oldham, John	BK07

P

Palmer, Arnold	S14
passion	BK26, S03
peace	Golf11, Golf12
Perry, Kenny	Golf17
perseverance	BB02, BB05, BK13, Golf07, Golf19
Phelps, Michael	BB02, S26, S31
Piccolo, Brian	FB10
Player, Gary	Golf18
prayer	FB08, Golf18, Golf20
prophecy	Golf26
Prophecy, Messianic	S20
Prophetic Warnings	FB23
Pujols, Albert	BB10

R

repentance	BB15, BK09, BK19, BK31, Golf08, Golf22
respect	BK07
Richardson, Bobby	S01
Richt, Mark	FB27, Golf04
Rickey, Branch	BB20
Riley, Mykal	BK11, S22
Riley, Pat	BK09
Robinson, Jackie	BB20
Rockne, Knute	FB10
Rodgers, Johnny	FB17
Ruth, Babe	BB06

S

T

U

Unitas, Johnny	FB11

V

Veil of the Temple	FB21

W

Walker, Herschel	FB04, FB05, FB23, FB29
Walker, Jimmy	S01
Warner, Kurt	S04
Watson, Tom	Golf20
Webster, Marvin	BK01
Wilkins, Dominique	BK14
Woods, Tiger	Golf08, Golf11, Golf24, S10, S23
Wooldridge, Dan	BK30
Wubbena, Del	BK22

Y

Yang, Y. E.	S23
Youssef, Dr. Michael	S30

REFERENCES

BB04   *White Sox's Buehrle Pitches Perfect Game, Thanks to Wise's Catch,* http://www.cbssports.com/mlb/gametracker/recap/MLB_20090723_TB@CHW

BB06   *Curse of the Bambino,* http://wikipedia.com

BB09   *Jeff Francoeur Testimony,* Northeast Georgia FCA Banquet, January 2008

BB10   *GoodNewsInSports.blogspot.com, Albert Pujols Stays Humble,* July 28, 2007

BB11   *cbn.com, John Smoltz: The Search for Significance,* Will Dawson, *The 700 Club, August 21, 2006*

BB13   *Twelve Keys to an Effective Church,* Dr. Kenneth Callahan, pp.53–54

BB16   *Fever Pitch,* 2005, Directors: Bobby Farelly, Peter Farrelly, Writers: Babaloo Mandel, Lowell Ganz, Nick Hornby http://en.wikipedia.org/wiki/Branch_Rickey

BB20   *Branch Rickey,* http://en.wikipedia.org/wiki/Branch_Rickey

BB24   *Sid Bream, Renowned Atlanta Braves 1st Baseman,* http://premierespeakers.com/christian/sid_bream/bio

BB24   *Skip Caray, Sid Bream,* wikipedia.com

BB25   *Ernie Banks,* wikipedia.com

BK01   *Marvin Webster,* wikipedia.com

BK05   *Maravich,* Wayne Federman and Marshall Terrill in collaboration with Jackie Maravich-McLachlan, pp. 356–358

BK09   *Three-peat,* wikipedia.com

BK17 *Maravich,* Wayne Federman and Marshall Terrill in collaboration with Jackie Maravich-McLachlan, pp. 76–77

BK21 *Pete Maravich Testimony,* Jimmy Walker video, Phoenix, AZ, October 9, 1985

BK22 *Maravich,* Wayne Federman and Marshall Terrill in collaboration with Jackie Maravich-McLachlan, p. 326, pp. 328–329, p. 342, p, 350

BK27 *Maravich,* Wayne Federman and Marshall Terrill in collaboration with Jackie Maravich-McLachlan, p.25

BK28 *Maravich,* Wayne Federman and Marshall Terrill in collaboration with Jackie Maravich-McLachlan, p. 323

BK31 *The Pistol,* Mark Kriegel, p. 132

FB04 Sports Illustrated, *More Than Georgia on His Mind,* Curry Kirkpatrick, August 31, 1981

FB07 *Me and Julio Down by the Schoolyard,* Paul Simon, 1972

FB12 *The Journey,* Billy Graham, p. 54

FB14 *Christian Examiner, Heisman Winner Has Priorities in Order,* Joni B. Hannagan, January 2008

FB15 *Forrest Gump the Movie,* 1994, Director: Robert Zemeckis, Created by Winston Groom

FB20 *Aggie Bonfire,* wikipedia.com

FB26 *fca.org, Life's Playbook, The Personal Testimony of Tony Dungy*

FB26 http://www.cbn.com/700club/features/TonyDungy_AllProDad_0610.aspx, *Tony Dungy, the All Pro Dad,* CBN Sports, by Shawn Brown

FB27 *http://www.uga.edu/teamunited/testimonies/mark_richt.htm, Mark Richt - UGA Football Head Coach*

FB27 http://www.familyfirst.net/press-room/press-releases/all-pro-dad-press-releases/tony-dungy-and-mark-richt-put-fatherhood-first/, *Tony Dungy and Mark Richt Put Fatherhood First*

FB28 *Sharing the Victory Magazine,* Fellowship of Christian Athletes, December 2002

FB29 *savannahnow.com, When Herschel Walker Speaks People Listen,* Tim Guidera, October 10, 2006

FB30 *BPSports.net, Football and Faith Are Big Business for Bobby Bowden,* Sandra Vidak, June 12, 2001

FB32 *A Simple Call,* Tommy Bowden, 1973

Golf01 *Facing the Giants the Movie,* 2006, directed by Alex Kendrick, written by Alex and Stephen Kendrick

Golf02 Golf Digest, September 2005 article, Michel Hepp'

Golf06, *Ben Hogan,* wikipedia.com

Golf09 *Links Players International, Reborn,* Bernhard Langer, Copyright 2007 Links Players International

Golf10 *Links Players International, Significance, Larry Mize,* Copyright 2007 Links Players International

Golf11 BPSports.Net, *After Winning the Masters, Johnson Credits the Master,* Art Stricklin, April 18, 2007

Golf12 Taken from *Payne Stewart: The Authorized Biography* by Tracey Stewart with Ken Abraham, hopeway.com, Christian Ditchfield, Copyright ©2000 by Anastasia T. Stewart. Used by permission of Broadman & Holman Publishers.

Golf13 *The Christian Index, Georgia Baptist golfer Nelson to be inducted into World Golf Hall of Fame,* J. Gerald Harris, October 26, 2006

Golf14 Taken from *Zinger, www.preachhim.org/Christiandeath.htm. Resurrection Promises, Preaching Today,* Robert Russell, May 9, 2008

Golf15 *The Christian Index, Stewart Cink: Premier Golfer, Christian gentleman, missionary volunteer,* J. Gerald Harris, January 6, 2005

Golf16 *Links Players International, I Felt Like a Failure,* Tom Lehman, 2007 Copyright Links Players International

Golf17 *masters.org, The 2009 Masters Golf Tournament,* April 13, 2009

Golf17 *Kenny Perry's Old Kentucky Home–3 Tours & News, http://www. golf.com/golf/tours_news/article/0.28136,1839965–3.00.html*

Golf18 *charlotteobserver.com,* Ron Green Jr., April 11, 2009

Golf19 *The Augusta Chronicle, Broadcaster Pat Summerall shares faith at Masters breakfast, Kelly Jasper, April 7, 2009*

Golf27 *What a day, what a Masters*, by Doug Roberson and Furman Bisher, AJC, April 12, 2009

Golf27 *Bobby Jones*, http://en.wikipedia.org/wiki/Bobby_Jones_(golfer)

S01   Crain, October 2, 2008, http://stevecrain.blogspot.com/2008/10/bobby-richardson-and-mickey-mantle_02.html

S01   *Pete Maravich Testimony*, Jimmy Walker video, Phoenix, AZ, October 9, 1985

S06   http://answers.yahoo.com/question/index?qid=2009020 4003914AAuSuK, *Renew a Steadfast Spirit Within Me*, Vonette Bright

S13   http://www.soccerballworld.com/1930%20Soccer%20Ball.htm

S14   *Pete Maravich Testimony*, Billy Graham Crusade video, Columbia, SC, April 1987

S23   *Max McGee*, wikipedia.com

S26   *Usain Bolt*, wikipedia.com

S30   *"Signed, Sealed, Delivered,"* Stevie Wonder, 1970, wikipedia.com

S30   MercyMe, *"Spoken For"* by MercyMe, writer Bart Millard, mercyme.com, 2002